POWER-SELLING
BY TELEPHONE

Barry Z. Masser

&

William M. Leeds

Parker Publishing Company, Inc.

West Nyack, New York

© 1982, by

PARKER PUBLISHING COMPANY, INC.

West Nyack, N.Y.

10   9   8

Library of Congress Cataloging in Publication Data

Masser, Barry Z.
  Power-selling by telephone.

  Includes index.
  1. Telephone selling.   I. Leeds, William M.
II. Title.
HF5438.3.M37   658.8′5   81-14085
                                   AACR2

Printed in the United States of America

foreword

Sales leads are perishable. If you've ever tried to squeeze sales out of six-month-old direct mail responses, I don't have to convince you of that fact.

Whether you're a marketing executive in a large firm or the operator of a small business, you know that the inquiries you generate by advertising, referrals, trade shows, "cold calls," and other means *must be* followed up quickly and courteously, with pertinent data.

Efficient sales lead follow-up is my business. Since 1966, my company has grown to a point where over a million inquiries a year are processed for more than 140 clients. And while telephone selling should be an integral part of any total inquiry-handling system, I could never personally endorse a phone selling program . . . until now.

Authors Barry Masser and Bill Leeds provide telephone sales consulting to many of the same accounts my firm services and to a large number of other companies. I've seen them in action, and I know their methods *work.* Here are a few reasons why I believe this telephone selling system of theirs has achieved national recognition:

- The techniques are highly structured. As a result, they keep the caller solidly on-track all the way through the close.

- The ingenious structure recommended by Masser and Leeds is easy to learn and just as easy to actually deliver to prospects in a relaxed, natural way. The presentation comes across professionally, and it gets results.
- The program is modular, so you can use just the parts *you* need to sell more effectively. And you can readily adapt the modules to fit any product or service, simple or complex. This flexibility lets you effectively reach any level of prospective buyer with equal comfort, from clerk to company president.

What really sold me was this: the authors claim that their telephone selling system is four times more effective than traditional sales methods. According to statistics I've seen, that claim is not exaggerated.

Mike Simon, President
Inquiry Handling Service, Inc.
Sylmar, California

how this book
will increase
your sales and profits

Here's a fact that *no* astute business person would challenge today:

> *A properly designed telephone sales program, undertaken by an individual or business that did not previously sell by phone, can quickly yield up to a four-time increase in sales and profits. This is true for virtually any company—large or small— that sells a product or service!*

In calling campaigns that we have designed and implemented (each program based *precisely* on the same methods described in later pages), *70 percent increases in business activity are typical!* The really astonishing thing about the power of telephone selling is this: It works even in the face of serious dilemmas confronting practically *all* businesses. Dilemmas like these:

The Travel Crunch. High travel costs may prevent salespeople from visiting their prospects and keep retail shoppers at home, but telephone selling *demolishes* the high cost of travel and puts the seller right back in command of profit generation.

Unproductive Field Sales Calls. With the cost of a field sales call in most markets averaging over $150, salespeople can't *afford* to call on any but the most ready-to-buy prospects. The telephone reveals in seconds who the real buyers are.

Fierce Competition. Tough rivals seem to spring up constantly. It's probably an ongoing headache in *your* business, too. But telephone selling gets *you* to the buyers first. *It never* fails to provide a clear competitive edge!

An Erratic World Economy. The fluctuating economy has turned basic business survival into a grinding challenge. Sales downturns wreck many firms, but the positive economics of telephone selling can make you and your business all but immune to those unpredictable fluctuations.

There isn't any question that the telephone can accomplish dramatic results. In just a matter of days, it can bring *you* the same remarkable benefits that hundreds of other sellers are enjoying right now. The following samples are taken from the dozens of highly detailed case histories you'll find as you read *Power-Selling By Telephone:*

There are literally thousands of people like Lonnie W.—individuals who invest every cent they have to open a small retail shop or service business. More than 80 percent of them fail. But Lonnie used (and still uses) the telephone to gain quick and absolute success for his modest gift shop. *His* caller generated sales of $1,900 in just five days . . . for the same cash outlay a meaningless ad would have cost him! See Chapter 1 for his complete story.

Celia sells real estate in a brutally competitive area

But she's a consistent sales leader for this reason: Celia uses the *checklist* technique to *assure* that her telephone presentation is always brimming with color, drama, and points of tremendous interest to her prospects! See Chapter 2 for details.

Walt M. sells courses to top managers. His elusive prospects require *a specially structured telephone presentation and an extra potent Power-Close*. It's explained in Chapter 7.

In Chapter 12, you'll discover exactly how two manufacturers and a rental firm use *Teleblitz* zone-saturation calling to achieve phenomenal dollar volume.

Plus, you'll learn how to use the *Fog Index* and the *Rule of 100* to create telephone dialogue that commands prospect attention. You'll discover the *Power-Pause* . . . the *Shock Approach* and the *Re-entry* techniques that produce sales when conventional methods fail.

In each case, you'll see how breathtaking increases in sales and profits flow directly from telephone calling campaigns. And in every case, without exception, the individual or business follows a *definite master plan* that consists of . . .

- A *structured* telephone presentation that includes crucially important steps that *must be present in a successful telephone selling effort!*
- Planned dialogue that makes closing a sale the easiest, most natural thing you've ever done.
- *Backup data* that slices through a prospect's stalls and objections like a hot knife through butter.

In addition to a windfall of field-proven telephone selling dynamite, this unusual book also provides the how-to's of starting your own phone sales consulting business; little-known data on slashing long-distance charges by using alternative telephone services, and much, much more.

Whether you're a seller, a business owner and operator,

a manager, or a consultant, *Power-Selling By Telephone* is a *must* if you want to successfully compete today and during the uncertain years ahead.

Barry Z. Masser

William M. Leeds

table of contents

CHAPTER 2

Building a Checklist That Lays the Base for Phenomenal Telephone-Selling Results 41

CHAPTER 3

How to Build a Powerhouse Six-Step Telephone Presentation 51

CHAPTER 4

Zero In on the Hot Telephone Prospects Fast By Qualifying Them! 63

CHAPTER 5

Putting a Ton of Punch Into Your Telephone Power-Selling Program 75

CHAPTER 6

Inside Technique Tips from America's Leading Telephone Money-Makers 91

CHAPTER 7

Penetrating Tough Defenses to Sell Top-Level Decision Makers By Telephone 105

CHAPTER 8
Fail-Safe Telephone Sales Approaches That Close Tough Customers 121

CHAPTER 9
Merchandising Strategies That Guarantee Big-Profit Orders By Phone 133

CHAPTER 10

Phone-Selling Controls to Build an Automatic Business-Producing Machine 147

CHAPTER 11

A Foolproof Telephone Follow-up System That Automatically Builds a Backlog of New Sales . 167

CHAPTER 12

Teleblitz: An Extraordinary Telephone Approach for Building Major Sales **179**

CHAPTER 13

Multiply Your Income with a Telephone Sales Business of Your Own **197**

CHAPTER 14
A Mini-Management Manual for Telephone
Sales Professionals 215

how major corporations and small businesses are cashing in by telephone

1

Telephone selling is an amazingly potent selling force *for every kind of business— for any product or service.*

There is absolutely no question that a properly planned and structured calling program will skyrocket your sales and profits. And with those dramatic results, it will also bring you *instant success* in these vitally important areas:

1. Using the telephone for selling or setting qualified field appointments will *dramatically lower your field sales costs* so that the effects of high travel costs are all but neutralized!

2. You'll *beat your toughest competitors* consistently by using the telephone intelligently. You get the big orders before your rivals even know they're available!

3. You'll *guarantee* for yourself *a steady and growing repeat business.* It happens automatically when you utilize the power of telephone selling.

4 You'll *eliminate slack selling seasons* by filling your
   sales "pipeline." You'll give unsurpassed service by
   being there when your customers want you and
   when their needs develop. And you'll benefit in
   scores of other ways, all thoroughly described in
   these pages.

In this opening chapter, we'll survey a cross section of firms
that are profiting through power-selling by telephone.

How Travel Costs Drove Maury G.'s
Sales Expenses Through the Roof—
and How He Lowered Them

Of all the factors that were multiplying the cost of
doing business for this insurance man, the accelerating
price of travel led the way. Maury G.'s informal figures
showed that getting a signed contract cost him around $175
two years ago, and was up to nearly $300 today, with no
relief in sight.

Maury's average $500 commission was eroding at an
alarming rate by the increased cost of driving, more expensive support help in his office, doubled advertising rates, and
scores of other items.

The procedure Maury successfully utilized was simple
and straightforward. Leads flowed in from direct mail and
newspaper ads They arrived steadily, in quantities that
kept Maury extremely busy. There were so many, in fact,
that he paid personal visits only to those in neighborhoods
convenient to his office. The others received a brochure describing his company's various insurance plans, then were
permanently filed away and forgotten.

During the course of an average day, Maury visited and
presented his deal to six prospects. Of these, three usually
turned out to be genuine sale possibilities. His ratios showed
that one of the three were eventually closed. At about $335
profit, one close a day wasn't bad. But at the more recent

margin of $200 or so, Maury was slipping rapidly into trouble.

If all six of the daily visits could be made to better-quality prospects, the number of closes would rise to three (assuming the one-third ratio held true). To do that, Maury would have to change his methods rather drastically; he would have to contact every inquiry to get a reading on readiness-to-buy. Then personal appointments would be set with those well-qualified leads, and each day would be devoted exclusively to personal visits with only these "hot" prospects.

The old "see only the convenient leads" policy was quickly discarded.

Maury's secretary agreed to reach all incoming ad responses by phone and to set up field appointments with the qualified ones. It worked: Within 30 days, *average daily revenues were up to $560!*

You Can't Afford to Chase Smoke Stacks!

Maury had settled into the wasteful habit of spending too much of his valuable time on *nonbuyers*. To make matters worse, he disregarded many promising inquiries that were not geographically convenient to his business. He got away with these lazy selling procedures as long as he could generate a relatively fat profit from just one insurance contract. But when expenses started climbing, Maury felt the pinch.

Here's the brutal truth:

> *With today's travel problems—plus other factors that drive the cost of a sale out of sight—you have to limit your personal sales visits only to highly qualified prospects who you know are close to buying.*

You simply cannot afford to run all over the map looking for that proverbial needle in the haystack.

The telephone allows you to find out quickly who your hot prospects are, and who the time-wasting "tire-kickers" are. This does not mean that you simply throw away the leads that do not seem ready to buy right now. They are merely handled differently from the hot ones. They are classified by you in terms of readiness-to-buy, then put into a follow-up system (described in Chapter 11) that assures the greatest possible conversion to orders at some time in the future.

Let's concentrate on *immediate* profits right now.

Telephone Qualifying: A Quick Way for Anyone to Become Up to Three Times More Time and Profit-Effective

The words above are *not* just one more attention-getting claim without basis in fact. The truth is that, when used according to this power-selling system, the telephone will increase, by a *factor of three*, the sales productivity of virtually *any* individual or corporation.

This dramatic fact has been so widely proven and so extensively documented over a period of so many years that its validity is undeniable. It works for the smallest one-person businesses all the way up to America's giant corporations. To *you,* it might mean something like this:

> *If you've been earning $15,000 a year in field sales by visiting your prospects, the telephone can quickly skyrocket that figure to $45,000 or more!*

Or, if you're a marketing executive with responsibility for making sales, increasing profits, and controlling expenses, it could mean something like this:

> *The telephone will give you rapid sales supremacy over your toughest competitors* (assuming they are not as adept in telephone selling as you are). *The results will be vastly better profits. Your*

sales costs will shrink because phoning is inexpen-
sive. Other expenses will be controlled because you
all but eliminate visits to prospects with poor order
potential!

Telephone selling can make the difference between a
marginal income and a fabulous one. It can turn an adequate
sales department into one that's an industry leader!

Why is telephone up to three times more potent than
personally visiting prospects? Simply because telephone
enables you to cover that much more ground!

A salesperson might be able to drop in on four leads a
day. (Let's say five for the sake of discussion.) A telephone
user, however, can reach 15 prospects a day. In other words,
exactly *three times more reach!*

Now, what happens the *next* day? The salesperson who
visits goes on five more personal visits to unqualified leads.
He'll get an order here and an order there. But the *telephone
caller* goes on five highly qualified field sales appointments
that were arranged by phone, and easily closes *twice* the
number of orders that his counterpart does.

In addition to closing more effectively, the phone user
reaches *all* inquiries quickly, thus beating competitors to the
draw. The visitor watches most leads fall to his or her rivals
because the inquiries just can't be worked on fast enough!

When you look at increased production of that kind on a
company-wide basis, you *really* see dramatic results. Here's
an example of one such instance.

How a High-Technology Firm Turns
Thin Dimes Into $50,000 Orders

The founder of F Company is an electronics wizard. He
invented an advanced (and very costly) electronics component in a rented one-room workshop. With his last few dollars, he hired a salesman and sent him out to visit companies
that appeared to be solid prospects.

The product was an instant success despite its huge price tag. The sales organization grew to 23 people in 18 months. Each person *still* followed the original method and *personally* called on firms that appeared to have need of the product.

By the third year of operation, two competitive firms had grown into formidable factors and were making serious inroads into F Company's market. While there was still a backlog of unfilled orders on-hand, dark clouds were on the horizon.

The company owner finally responded. He hired a new Marketing Manager and gave strict instructions to institute immediately an intensive telephone-calling campaign to set field sales appointments. The new executive created a presentation, acquired a good prospect list, and then set the wheels in motion.

Every salesperson would spend two hours per day calling firms in his or her territory. The remainder of each day would be spent demonstrating products to *qualified* buyers. *No more time was to be squandered on personal visits to cold leads!*

In 60 days, F Company was well on its way to the top again. This surge was largely attributable to the fact that expensive salespeople were no longer chasing hundreds of bad prospects to find a few good ones. But equally important was that *competitors were now being beaten to the punch.*

A few statistics gathered by F Company in its phenomenally successful new telephone campaign should be interesting to you.

Some Shocking Figures About How Good Leads Are Wasted

The following chart (Figure 1-1) depicts eye-opening statistics revealed by recent independent research.

As Figure 1-1 shows, many companies could be missing up to *40 percent* of their potential sales!

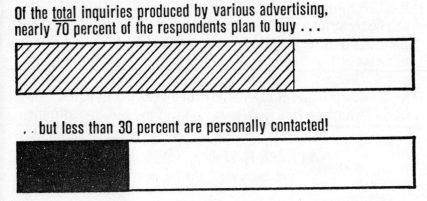

Figure 1-1

F Company had been losing ground to competitors for two reasons:

1. Because their salespeople were instructed to contact prospects only on a personal basis, they were talking to *only 30 percent of the company's total potential market!* Running around in heavy traffic is *not* conducive to identifying genuine prospects.

The acquisition of an up-to-date prospect list quickly revealed how many likely buyers there really were across the nation. The owner's overly conservative marketing approach had come uncomfortably close to causing havoc.

Use of the telephone at F Company puts the company in touch with an estimated 92 percent of its market. And F Company is covering all that ground very nicely, very rapidly.

2. Of the 30 percent market portion that the company's salespeople *were* covering, *nearly half* was being lost to the two competitors. Why? Because follow-up visits were made far too late, *if at all*. The salespeople were closing a few deals on initial sales calls, but if more work was needed, one or both of the rivals would come swooping down to get the order.

A telephone follow-up system at F Company has cut the

loss to competitors down to 4 percent. If necessary, a prospect can be recalled on a daily basis until the sale is finalized. The time it takes for such an intensive follow-up is only a few minutes a day.

F Company's success is a striking example of how virtually any product can benefit through telephone sales. Now let's see how an *intangible* service can be sold by calling.

A Fortune Is Waiting on the Line for Service Companies

Intangible and *conceptual* selling are frightening terms to many professional salespeople. If they can't touch or smell something, it can't be adequately described. And if it can't be described, how can it be effectively marketed?

The truth is, intangible services are *especially* well-suited for telephone selling. Some of the most drama-packed presentations are built around services that are extremely difficult to define in a few words. A later chapter includes examples of these.

Insurance policies, tax shelter investments, and other intangibles have been sold in record numbers, even *without* personal contact between seller and buyer. At the same time this huge volume of business is being rung up by telephone, thousands of intangible-product salespeople are still pounding the pavement. They insist on doing it the hard way—and continue to lose ground to those who believe in dialing!

The next story typifies the kind of success you can expect by building a strong telephone presentation around a hard-to-sell concept.

Don K.'s Plant Security Agency Goes Statewide in Just Eight Months

Don K. started in a 12-by-8-foot office with a file cabinet and telephone. That was *all* he needed to propel his agency into an industry leadership role, and into profitability that Don wouldn't have imagined possible just one year earlier.

As a former law enforcement officer, Don knew of the tremendous need in factories and warehouses for strong security. But in laying the groundwork for his new business, he never gave serious consideration to the necessity of *marketing* his new service. Like the proverbial "better mousetrap," he believed that new clients would beat a path to his door. This unbelievably naive position nearly led to the failure of his enterprise.

On the strength of a small ad in the local classified telephone directory, plus a few thousand mailers to local companies, Don sat back and waited for calls. In four weeks, he received a total of three inquiries. One looked like a possible client, but wouldn't begin to think about a definite decision for another six months or more. Therefore, the first dollar of income hadn't yet arrived, but expenses continued to mount.

Out of desperation and boredom, Don began calling prospects. His first attempts were purely ad lib; Don spoke spontaneously, with no preconceived idea about what direction the call would take. On top of that, he called blindly, without any notion of who in the firm made security decisions.

But there *were* early successes. The first week of calling yielded four appointments with interested firms. Of these, one solid client resulted. The following week, he increased his number of appointments and added two more closes. Most important, every time Don came upon an effective phrase—or better way of handling himself in a selling call—*he wrote it down.*

By month four, Don was too busy seeing clients to continue calling. So he tried a full-time telephone salesperson and trained him in the techniques he had developed. By his eight-month anniversary, Don's client base was statewide, and he had opened branch offices in key regions to control his growing business.

What did Don say about his service to make it so appealing? Here's a look at how the trial-and-error program evolved—and turned into a powerhouse vehicle for selling intangible services.

Giving Intangibles Overwhelming Appeal

Don learned the hard way. He faced the necessity of getting his security service off the ground through *direct telephone contact.* This was the only way left to him after the failure he had experienced through other means. He had to make telephone soliciting work without the benefit of a book like this one that could show him how to do it.

During those first weeks of building a presentation, Don established these rules for selling his intangible service:

1. To deal with anyone below the company owner or chief executive officer is a waste of time. It is okay to be *referred* to a subordinate by the top person, but *starting* with a low-level employee generally gets you nowhere fast.

2. Prospects are rarely interested in security companies as such, but *will* respond when the conversation centers on safeguarding a firm's assets. The "sizzle" has to be stressed, *never* the "steak."

3. A major service like Don's cannot actually be closed over the telephone. Don has to build up the prospect's appetite for *more information.* In essence, Don uses the phone to obtain an appointment for further discussion, and nothing more.

4. Pressure can *never* be used in going for an appointment. Although Don's normal style can be considered low key, he still proceeds extra cautiously in terms of applying pressure.

Now, let's take a quick look at the value of telephone selling for business *start-up* situations.

How Small Companies
Become Incredible Money-Makers

Why do some start-up enterprises succeed immediately while others fail? To carry that question a step further, why do certain average business concepts make it while many outstanding ideas do not?

The answer, to a significant extent, depends upon *exposure*. When the market is made aware of a new product or service, sales will ensue. But if the start-up company sits back and waits for buyers to discover them, failure inevitably results.

Exposure is available through direct mail and media advertising . . . often at a substantial cost. A solidly capitalized firm can handle the gigantic expenses associated with saturation ad campaigns—but the "shoestring" operation just can't compete in that game.

Thousands of brand-new enterprises fail every year because the owners never see that the telephone, sitting idly on their desk, holds the solution to gaining fast exposure, and the key to their dreams of business success!

In the following case, a retail start-up, decidedly average in every respect, rose to quick prosperity by virtue of the owner's resourcefulness and imagination.

How Lonnie W.'s Modest Store
Outgrosses Formidable Competition

Lonnie W. invested just over $5,000 for inventory (mid-priced gift items), $2,750 for rent and basic fixtures, and a nominal sum for a few other bare necessities. Thus, for an investment totaling less than $10,000, Lonnie was attempting to compete with well-established neighborhood stores.

Within the first week, the new owner came to these startling conclusions:

1. His shop would *not* benefit significantly from shopper traffic flowing to nearby stores as Lonnie thought it would. People passed enroute to the showrooms of competitors and rarely even glanced in his window.

2. Extremely low prices didn't make much of a difference. Customers never got close enough to find out about Lonnie's discounts!

3. The few modest ads Lonnie could afford did not come close to paying for themselves in added profits. They were overwhelmed by big ads bought by chain operations on the street.

Things changed *fast* the day a neighborhood telephone directory was delivered to the store. There in front of Lonnie was a listing of some 18,000 households in the immediate vicinity. *The very market* he so desperately needed was packed into those pages!

The next day, Lonnie's teenage daughter came in and started calling the "A" listings. She delivered a 40-second message that imparted these basic points:

1. The fact that the gift store was new and offered grand-opening specials.

2. A quick description of the general type of merchandise on display.

3. A bonus offer: If the person made *any* purchases within the next five days, a free surprise gift would be given.

Over the first five days of telephone calling, 70 calls a day resulted. Out of a total of 350 calls, 39 sales were directly attributed to this effort; a total dollar volume of nearly $1,900. Equally important, Lonnie's customer base was firmly established! It was a strong initial thrust.

The Telephone: A Certain Path to Prosperity for Retailers

Any store can instantly start cranking out new sales by telephone as Lonnie did. Almost any retail proprietor will confirm the fact that *waiting for customers* is the most mind-numbing pastime in that huge industry. Yet, only a handful of the people in that business utilize their unproductive time to generate new customers by phone (or any other way).

Thousands of store owners and managers depend on costly ads or inefficient in-store promotions to carry the *entire* load of business development. Salaried store salespeople sit around and stare at the front door, hungrily waiting for "walk-ins" or shoppers responding to ads.

Just 20 calls a day by an otherwise idle salesperson can dramatically boost sales. The results show up in one working week or less! If the regular sales crew is busy with other tasks, a telephone salesperson can be hired at budget rates to handle the ongoing program.

If you are a retailer looking for ways to skyrocket sales and profits, *look to the telephone.* It's the most economical and hardest-hitting advertising medium you possess! Here's an instance where phoning propelled a newly-opened automobile dealership to strong sales.

A Fast Path to Industry Leadership: How the Phone Did It for Mel B.

Back when Mel B. worked as a used car salesman, he learned two things that were to guide his business future:

1. Almost every family owns at least one automobile.
2. Rather than being just a necessity, that family car (or cars) is often a subject of near adoration—particularly to the men.

Although these solidly established facts were well known to almost every salesperson in the industry, virtually all car agencies saw commissioned employees waiting around for lookers to drop in. Mel was flabbergasted; he was positive that most serious drivers would be delighted to talk cars. And, following such talk, many would be receptive to talking about a deal.

With that theory strongly in mind—and with financial help from his family—Mel started his own new car dealership.

As soon as equipment was in place and staffing was completed, Mel and a commissioned salesperson started calling. They worked from three customer lists they bought from local auto supply stores; their objective was to reach obvious car enthusiasts and invite them to test drive the new agency's two-seater import.

The following pattern quickly emerged. Of every ten people actually contacted, three expressed a desire to see the car. Since the two men were each able to make 30 calls in the course of an evening, that yielded eighteen interested prospects. Four of the eighteen visited the dealership, and one of these would eventually convert to a sale (over $15,000 in gross).

The ratios held amazingly steady. In the first two weeks of operation, 12 car sales were attributed to the phone campaign. By adding to that, orders generated by other advertising, the business was off to a booming start.

As time went on, Mel and his cohort found that the press of business prevented their continued personal participation in the calling program. So a secretary was trained to use the presentation, and the thrust went on as before. His agency is today one of the region's most profitable and efficient. Mel's operation passed a powerful and well-established competitor after only ten months from the day he opened for business!

As you'll see right now, the telephone is a formidable way to neutralize strong business rivals.

Dealing Competition a Kayo
Without Knocking Them

Back when Mel was a commissioned new car salesman, some of his biggest headaches came from competitive auto dealers. Potential customers would enter the showroom armed with quotations from every rival auto agency within a hundred-mile radius. Mel understood that by *passively waiting* for shoppers, each salesperson was losing the initiative; every one of them was in a *defensive* position—*not* on the *offensive* as an effective seller must be.

The telephone was the key to moving back on the offensive. By identifying prospects *before they entered the competitive market,* Mel seized the initiative right away, and usually *kept* it!

The people Mel called to invite in for a test drive were not strongly aware of rival agencies; therefore, he had an opportunity to close the deal without serious interference from every rival in town.

Calling is the quickest way to beat competitors to the punch. And it's done *without* knocking or downgrading them in any way. Using the telephone to locate prospects is like getting a big head start in a footrace!

Beating rivals to the prize is one enormous advantage to calling. But another is your power to assure the ongoing integrity of customers you've already sold. The following shows how this works.

Commanding Customer Loyalty By Telephone

When a business is purchased, the new owners often pay a substantial price for *goodwill*. Fixtures, inventory and accounts receivable can be quantified easily enough, but the value of an established customer base (goodwill) can be of incalculable worth.

Most business operators are guilty of gross neglect when it comes to providing service to current buyers. They are apparently unaware of these facts:

1. In some industries, a satisfied customer can provide five or more referrals per month. That, for all practical purposes, is free business.

2 Most minor customer grievances are never communicated to the owner or manager of a company. The problem festers, and the consumer goes elsewhere when the time to buy arrives again. Also, this quietly suffering person will very likely steer friends *away* from the unsuspecting firm

The typical manager wrongly assumes that once a sale is made, a customer has been added and that customer will automatically buy again and again. The boss turns the focus of attention elsewhere, and erosion begins.

Routine calling of present customers will not only stop the loss of customers, but will assure tremendous referral activity.

This is true no matter what kind of product or service you deal in. Such a program should be pursued as vigorously as a new business acquisition, since the results can easily *equal* or *surpass* new sales.

By intelligently cultivating a modest customer base, the following office supply salesperson regularly outproduces more experienced people.

How Sales Beginner Ada S. Consistently Outruns Her Rivals

When Ada S. first joined a large office supply firm as a junior sales representative, she was given one of the least promising territories in the city—and a list of some 35 present and past customers.

She noticed immediately that the more senior salespeople in the organization concentrated on opening new accounts. Promotional mailers went out to all customers on a monthly basis, and everyone assumed that this was enough to assure repeat orders and loyalty.

Ada didn't agree. She knew that those previously sold accounts held the greatest promise of fast, substantial business. Prospecting for *new* sales would indeed be taken care of, but would *not* be emphasized to the exclusion of everything else—as it was with most of the other sales reps.

Her strategy took shape this way: On a typical day, Ada would telephone no less than seven old accounts. The balance of her time would be devoted to acquiring new business. Assuming normal growth of her customer base, this method of attack would put Ada in personal touch with each buyer at least once every two weeks.

Such a concerted follow-up effort was unheard of in her company; it was considered gross overkill by the veteran sales types. But she proceeded without hesitation. On her second day after training, Ada received the first payoff. A long inactive account gave her a telephone order for three file cabinets and a desk. Her call just happened to jibe with a rapidly developing need in the client company. By the end of that same week, she had written over $1,000 in orders, all from those 35 prior accounts considered dormant by her firm's management!

While Ada continued to harvest big repeat orders from old accounts, she was also able to maintain a respectable pace adding *new* clients. The bottom line was this: Ada consistently outproduced the high-earning oldtimers in the company. *The telephone proved to be the weapon of superiority*.

This saleswoman's approach gave her one more distinct advantage over intercompany rivals. Here's a look at why this approach works.

The Incomparable Power
of Lead-Independence

Ada S. does not depend on her employer for lead-generating programs. Mel B., the car dealer, simply will not tolerate salespeople who ask for heavy advertising to build shopper-traffic. Lonnie W. confidently turns down most publications that solicit him for ad space. Don K.'s security service is thriving without the benefit of expensive media buys. F Company grosses millions a year, but maintains a remarkably small budget for publicity.

The telephone has taken over the burden of lead generation for these individuals and businesses and countless others all over America. Each one is *lead-independent,* and that adds up to the following:

1. Their budgets for advertising are *minimal.* While ads are extremely valuable and work hand-in-hand with telephone selling, the expense for ads today is horrendous and rising steadily. Budgets *must* be reduced to help obtain lower cost-of-sales. This is doubly critical for small, start-up businesses.

2. Being lead-independent virtually eliminates poor response periods during holiday seasons. When most firms tighten their belts certain times each year, telephone-oriented companies continue cranking out sales. There are no serious lulls or slumps for those who create their own qualified leads.

3. Companies that offer a variety of products or services can control sales volume. They can increase orders for a selected item and decrease activity on another at will. Thus, they can control inventory and sell according to production capability. For example, a slow-selling product can be pitched strongly by phone and liquidated in record time.

4. Companies that suffer with certain weak territories (and nearly all of them have that problem) can use a tele-

phone "blitz" campaign in those regions. It builds sales as rapidly as it can be handled.

In essence, the telephone can be likened to a faucet that you, the marketer, can turn on or off as desired. It *eliminates* your dependence on outside forces that may or may not work in your favor.

From this point on, we'll get into the building of a power-selling telephone program. The first step is to gather essential facts.

building a checklist that lays the base for phenomenal telephone-selling results

2

Before you can even begin to construct a power-selling program, you have to collect high-quality data about your product or service.

That appears to be a simple enough undertaking, but it's amazing how many companies—some of them giants— don't have good information about their products immediately accessible. Too often, the situation looks like this:

- The sales manager has some of the most important features and benefits . . . in his head.
- The controller has strong arguments about operating economics . . . in a desk drawer.
- The service manager understands various durability and wear facts . . . but does not freely communicate them.
- The engineers and designers know that superior materials and production techniques are utilized . . . but don't think anyone else cares about them.

While most of these details do get published in brochures and other promotional materials, it is a rare instance when *all* the facts are brought together on one desk top.

Your first step, the *checklist, assures* that you'll collect all the bits and pieces that are worth knowing. When that is accomplished, you'll possess the cornerstone of a superior product story.

Categories That Get to the Heart of Your Objectives

To effectively flush out the most appealing information about your product, you have to ask carefully-designed questions.

If *you* alone are the designer, manufacturer, and sales force for your firm, you obviously ask *yourself* the *checklist* questions. If you're in a corporate environment, get your key people together and ask *them* the questions. The point is that you *collect this crucial data from the people most qualified to provide accurate, clear data about what you are after.*

If necessary (and it usually is), you also consult the following sources, whenever available:

- Technical data sheets
- Ads on the product or service
- Any previously prepared training manuals
- Press releases, brochures, and point-of-purchase materials
- Annual reports, customer testimonials, etc.

Your ultimate objective is to learn everything you can about these vital areas:

1. Outstanding features and benefits
2. Critical disadvantages

3. How the product or service stacks up to that of leading competitors

4. Facts on initial and ongoing operating costs

5. Leading applications

6. Most identifiable markets

7. Delivery and service

8. Most common objections of prospects

9. Current marketing methods and means of distribution

10. Key qualifications of the typical individual who does the buying

11. Market conditions or trends that may enhance demand for the product or service

12. What the main goal would be in selling it by telephone (close, field appointment, or some other end result)

Next is the actual checklist used by a medical equipment salesman in putting together his highly successful telephone presentation.

Nineteen Questions That Led Nick R. to a Blockbuster Telephone Presentation

It took Nick most of one afternoon to locate and question the people who could best provide the input he needed. But the effort eventually paid off by providing the guts of his extremely strong telephone presentation.

When Nick finished, he had filled 15 legal-sized sheets of tightly written longhand notes. Out of this, he filtered out the facts that convinced some of the toughest buyers in the industry: hospital administrators and physicians.

Here are the 19 questions he asked (not necessarily in the sequence that they occurred):

1. If only *one* outstanding attribute of the x-ray machine could be considered, what would it be? (Tell in as few words as possible.)

2. List all other features and benefits that clearly stand out (in order of their perceived importance by users).

3. Why is this brand superior to those made by competitors?

4. What do competitors say about this unit?

5. What are the prices of all available configurations, and how do these prices compare with competitive units?

6. How do operating expenses compare?

7. Can time and cost savings be quantified?

8. What is delivery time?

9. What are the *realities* of field service?

10. Describe the optimum target market, and provide a composite of the typical target decision maker.

11. What are the most frequently occurring objections:
    a. from prospects?
    b. from users?

12. List the most valid applications for the unit. Get customer testimonials that support these applications.

13. Is anything occurring now in the medical field that would either enhance or diminish acceptance of the system?

14. How much technical data does the decision maker need before ordering?

15. Is technical backup expertise available immediately, if required?

16. Is *all* published material about the unit in my possession?

17. Is all competitive literature in my possession?
18. Are special promotions planned that might maximize my telephone program?
19. What is my primary objective in making telephone calls:
    a. To set a strong field sales appointment?
    b. To close the sale during the initial contact?
    c. To obtain some other desired result?

The abundance of product information that the above checklist evoked for Nick contained a few especially strong points. Now, he had to sift through the raw facts to isolate and refine those points.

Rating Data in Terms of Its Selling Power

In reviewing the notes you end up with after going through your checklist, adequate time has to be taken in identifying the points that will provide the real *firepower* for your presentation.

In distilling a page of rather mundane data into a handful of words that packed heavy punch, Nick used these general guidelines:

- Although manufacturing people gave him plenty of numbers and dimensions, Nick avoided including product specifications or other technical facts unless they represented clear benefits to a potential buyer—and could be easily identified as benefits by a nontechnical prospect.

- The Marketing Department provided comparisons, but the salesman avoided using any reference to competitive products, tempting as it was, when his equipment enjoyed obvious superiority in some areas.

- He searched for points that animated and dramatized his product.
- Without naming rival products, Nick selected any
  point that conveyed a distinct edge over similar
  products. In his case, this included lower initial cost,
  certain safety features that other x-ray units did not
  have, relative ease-of-use, and an excellent service
  program backed by local technicians.

Nick realized that his telephone presentation would
have to impart an extremely hard-hitting but clear message
in a matter of minutes. There was no room for information
that didn't have substantial impact. *All* superfluous details
were set aside by Nick as he sifted through the pages of notes
and quotes.

With some products or services, you have to search long
and hard to come up with a little excitement. In fact, you may
have to do a bit of work turning sawdust into gold dust, as
you'll see now.

Turning Ordinary Facts Into
Extraordinary Selling Impact

A company that does precision machining of critical
electromechanical parts wanted to reach its potential client
list by telephone to find out about future projects they might
bid on.

Two meetings of top-level people in the company failed
to produce agreement on how prospects could best be approached. Every presentation suggested was more ordinary
than the next. The marketing people wanted a little drama
and punch, but dry facts persisted to come forth.

Finally, someone suggested making a major point of the
firm's new computer-controlled machines; they permitted
consistently close tolerances and eliminated human error.
Only one other firm had this new technology, but wasn't

publicizing it. The concept was unanimously accepted. It provided the core of a very successful calling program.

Can anything be more sedate than group health insurance? It seems that many of the people who sell it are bored stiff with their own product. But Jerry V. is genuinely turned on by some of the features in the policies he carries.

When he cold-calls a prospective client, Jerry leads with machine-gun bursts of enthusiasm as he summarizes the best points in his program. He fully *expects* listeners to be as enthused as he is, and they often are.

When he applied the checklist concept to his major medical plan, certain distinct advantages came into focus, and Jerry used them in his remarkably effective telephone presentation.

Here's a top-earning real estate salesperson who uses the checklist concept on an almost daily basis.

Celia W. Shows How Basic Input Can Make a Winning Sales Campaign

Listings for houses and apartments for sale flow into Celia's real estate office almost daily. The usual practice was for an agent to call potential buyers and fill them in on the specifications of the available property.

What *should* have been an exciting and eventful telephone call for both the shopper and agent too often became a dull, colorless report of how many bedrooms and bathrooms the listing had.

Celia became convinced that much more drama and emotion could be built into every initial phone call. If a home purchase was, after all, the major event in many people's lives, the process leading up to that purchase had to be consistent with that importance.

The real estate woman began to screen every new listing personally. As she did so, the *dramatic* aspects of the property were summarized for the front-end of the telephone presentation.

Celia felt that if prospect *emotion* could be stirred in the first seconds of a call, the more mundane features could be presented later. She looked for emotional points that seemed to key into the known desires of specific prospects. A couple that had described a gardening hobby were greeted with:

". . . It's an English country rustic with a beautifully planted atrium and 28 trees of all descriptions."

A family involved in sports heard this opening:

". . . You'll have huge grounds for lots of physical activity. It has a den that would make a perfect trophy room—and you'd be two blocks from a recreation center!"

Needless to say, most of Celia's prospects had been qualified earlier as to their preferences. So the new checklist concept proved to be *especially* effective.

Turn Your Market Situation Into a Practical, Easy-to-Use Action Plan

Any business can come up with a drama-charged presentation, although some are more hard-pressed to dig out points of interest than others.

Most business operators and salespeople tend to say, "My product (or service) just isn't exciting. What can I say about it that will capture attention?" The following is a key to finding the answer to that question.

Briefly step back from your business—away from the day-to-day operational details. Look at it as objectively as you can. View it through the eyes of the people who buy its products or subscribe to its services.

Now try to *feel* what those customers feel; their desires, expectations, frustrations and anxieties; before, during, and after the actual purchase.

Every buyer (no matter what the purchased item happens to be) experiences anticipation first, then pride in the purchase. Too many salespeople forget that reactions like these occur, and therefore become quite emotionless about each transaction.

If you can go back and experience that almost childlike enthusiasm you had when you first started selling—and that you feel when you buy something you want—you can *easily* find exciting things to say about your wares!

When the strongest features and benefits have been successfully captured, your next step is to get them into an organized presentation format.

Fitting Your Selling Gems Into a Proven-Successful Structure

Your completed checklist is a strong first step toward building a telephone presentation that will make you more money. But it is just the groundwork. This collection of exceptionally convincing data will now be used as the bricks and mortar of your standard telephone presentation.

Your goal in doing this is to assure that *every* call you make gives you the best possible chance to close. In other words, you'll be delivering your best story *consistently.*

To fully understand that, look at it this way: Occasionally you have days when everything you say and do *works.* Somehow, your communications with prospects seem flawless, and the pieces just drop into place. But a day later, it's back to struggling for that certain magic; your words inexplicably change just a bit, and the small difference is enough to modify the end result.

The presentation in the next chapter is designed to make *every day an optimum day.* No more down periods, and measurably fewer slumps. By taking the most compelling features of your product, and *structuring* them logically, you'll be at your best every time you sell by phone!

Chapter 3 shows you how to do it.

how to build a powerhouse six-step telephone presentation

3

An accomplished golfer can split the fairway with booming drives on a reasonably consistent basis. In much the same way, a disciplined salesperson can deliver highly effective presentations time after time.

Both experts inevitably get off the track now and then. For the golfer, a slightly altered grip on the club shaft can introduce a slice that sends the ball into sand traps and rough. At the same time, a salesperson might inadvertently change the essential message, and prospects fail to respond as favorably as they had earlier.

A Step-by-Step Structured Approach to Unprecedented Earnings

The skillful golfer has a grooved, structured swing. Barely perceptible changes in stance or grip can be quickly identified. By the same token, a salesperson who uses a *structured presentation* is also in a kind of groove; the steps he or she uses have been *preestablished and logically se-*

quenced. Thus, unexpected flaws can be isolated and worked out almost immediately.

Since it's different from one day to the next, *an improvised or spontaneous approach* to golf or selling is difficult, if not impossible, to adjust or improve. Quality varies widely without apparent root cause. Therefore, *a structured approach to telephone selling is strongly recommended. It puts a sophisticated and proven set of strategies into an easy-to-use system.*

This chapter describes how to build and use the proven Six-Step Power-Selling Telephone Program.

How a Prepared Delivery
Gives Gerri T. Record Sales

Gerri is an Account Executive for a public relations firm. Early in her sales career she recognized that she was subject to severe mood changes. Erratic "ups and downs" were beginning to put her success outlook in question. A day of brilliant performance in phoning prospects would inevitably give way to a period of mediocre performances that would nullify the earlier gains.

Never an advocate of "canned pitches," Gerri nevertheless decided to standardize her basic telephone delivery. It seemed that doing so would protect her against the downswings. She would reconstruct the best phone presentations she could recall, and use the resulting model consistently, good mood or otherwise.

During this process, she learned of the power-selling method. A difficult task turned into a one-hour session. Gerri proceeded to use the structured approach in building her "ideal" telephone presentation, and it was easier to do than she ever imagined.

The results astonished her. During the first hours of use, it was a little clumsy not being as spontaneous as she always had been. But gradually the words and flow became comfortable. By the second day of calling, Gerri's typed presentation went into a nearby drawer. She was already delivering it confidently and naturally.

Most important, Gerri had all but eliminated those unpredictable low spots. Her prepared presentation brought about a 27 percent increase in new clients by the end of the third month. And it kept getting better for her as time went on.

Figure 3-1 is an illustration of the basic presentation structure used successfully by Gerri, hundreds of individual salespeople, and scores of large and small companies using the telephone to make more sales.

The Hard-Hitting Six-Step Program

Figure 3-1 shows the framework of the Six-Step Power-Selling Telephone Program, the one used so effectively for qualifying existing inquiries, and for generating sales from "cold" prospect lists.

Depending on what you are selling, a presentation built around this simple framework should run from four to seven minutes.

If you are wondering how such a straightforward flow of steps can take as long as seven minutes, remember that this is merely a *pattern* for the total presentation you will build for yourself. In actual practice, you'll have a *number* of qualification questions under Step 3 (as you'll see in Chapter 4) and a product or service description that, out of necessity, might be rather lengthy. In addition, any rebuttals you have to use in overcoming prospect objections can take time as well.

The finished presentation that evolves from this basic framework will be more complex than the illustration and will cover every obstacle you are likely to encounter along the path to a close.

Here's a brief rundown of what each step is about:

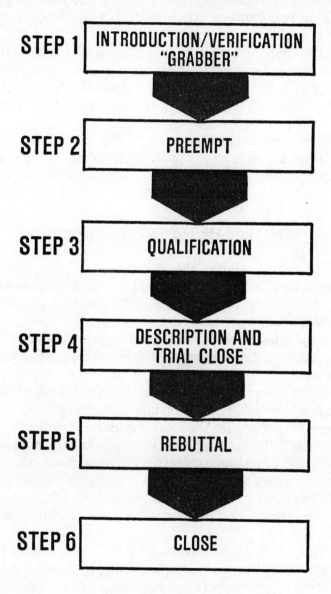

Figure 3-1

Step 1:
Introduction/
Verification/
"Grabber"

Very simply, announce who you are and the name of your company.

Next, be sure that the person you are talking to is the one you want. If you are working from inquiries that have been generated by advertising, you know who your contact should be. If "cold-calling," be certain your contact is someone who can make a buying decision.

The final phase of your introduction is a "grabber." This is a *very* brief but hard-hitting statement about your offer—just enough to spark prospect interest, but well short of the features and benefits rundown that you'll deliver in Step 4. An example of this is provided later in this chapter.

Step 2:
Preempt

In some cases, you can eliminate common prospect objections before they arise. This is possible if you have a situation where the same objections come up time after time. More about how to do this later in the chapter.

Step 3:
Qualification

Whether you go for the close on the first phone call, or use the call to set a strong field sales appointment, *your prospect must be pegged accurately before you agree to invest any more of your valuable time.* Qualification questions *will* reveal readiness-to-buy. It separates the *real* prospects from the lookers. Chapter 4 is devoted to the extremely important subject of qualifying.

Step 4:
*Description and
Trial Close*

In as few words as possible, describe the most significant advantages of your product or service. The language you develop has to sparkle like a diamond, and get right to the major prospect *hot buttons.* Immediately after the description, you subtly find out how near the prospect is to buying through use of a trial close. Chapter 5 shows how to develop an effective description.

Step 5:
Rebuttal

If your trial close draws resistance, *now* is the time to overcome that hurdle. You accomplish this by reaching for backup facts that pertain directly to the subject of the objection. Quite often, solid facts and figures can make resistance vanish. Using rebuttals to overcome objections is described later in this chapter.

Step 6:
Close

Asking for the order or for an appointment is a natural conclusion if all preceding steps have been accomplished as suggested. Chapter 7 gets into detail about effective telephone closes.

Starting now, we'll thoroughly explore each step of the presentation so you can easily build one of your own.

The Critically Important
Introduction/Verification/"Grabber"

In most instances, you'll be judged by a prospect before the first 15 words are out of your mouth. All sales relationships depend heavily on initial impressions. No matter how strong the ensuing steps happen to be, if your *opening* is weak or tentative, you'll be at a severe disadvantage the rest of the way.

While initial communications are crucial in terms of first impression, they are also the simplest steps in the presentation. They serve these basic purposes:

1. To convey your identity to the prospect.
2. To affirm that you are on the line with the person you want.
3. To dramatically let the individual know the reason why you are calling; thus, in a couple of brief words, you completely clear the air. You very effectively set the stage for the steps that follow. In actual practice, an introduction might take this shape. When your call is answered, you say. . . .

> "Hello . . . This is Jim Andrews, district sales representative for Apex Distributors. Am I speaking to Mr. Robert Hansen?"

> As soon as you have verified that your desired contact is on the line, you continue with a "grabber."

> "Your inquiry on the Model 2800 Transmitter a rived today. I'll give you information on that unit—plus the new 3000 which has 20 more channels and electronic tuning for only a few dollars more."

No beating around the bush—no skirting the issues. *Get right to the point!* Most prospects will appreciate this polite directness. *Salespeople who attempt to mask the fact that they are selling will inevitably fail.* The "grabber" conveys just enough provocative data to capture attention quickly.

Eliminating Objections Before They Come Up: How Cliff W. Disarms Prospects

Step 2, *the preempt,* is optional. It is invaluable in cases like the following one.

Cliff W. sells rental typewriter contracts. He competes against a well-established rental firm that specializes in a nationally advertised machine. When he first started in business, Cliff introduced himself by telephone, then, more often than not, received this response:

"We prefer the X machine because we're sure of getting quick service."

This objection immediately put Cliff on the defensive. Right off the bat, he found himself in a hole, futilely attempting to regain the initiative. But he rarely succeeded in overcoming that heavy blow.

Finally, the salesman decided to try a preemptive strategy. By delivering a service explanation *before* the prospect had a chance to bring it up, Cliff felt he could maintain control. Immediately after completing his introduction, this preempt followed:

"Nobody can beat our service in this region. We have same-day loaner machines, and usually your typewriter is returned to you in 48 hours or less."

Cliff's close ratio jumped 38 percent in 30 days. That *predictable* objection was effectively eliminated via the preemptive strategy.

Use this strategy *only* when you can count on getting resistance in certain areas. For example, if at least 50 percent of your phone calls draw a specific objection, by all means institute a preempt in Step 2! But if a basic objection comes up infrequently, deal with it only when you absolutely have to. This saves you the task of building a preempt into your presentation that you use in every call.

If you decide *not* to build in a preempt, you should at least be ready for the obstacles that a prospect may place in your path. Here's a way to remain a step ahead of those potential stumbling blocks.

Setting Up Escape Routes
That Get You Past Objections

For the purpose of illustration, let's say you encounter two objections repeatedly:

1. *Price resistance.*
2. *Delivery time complaints.*

While objections about price and delivery may come up frequently enough during the phone calls you make, let us say they don't, in your judgment, justify the addition of preempts to your telephone presentation. So you set up *escape routes* that you use *only when you need them.*

Here's one way of doing it: Instead of using Step 2 as a preempt, you use it as your *escape route* for the potential price and delivery sore spots. In your illustrated presentation framework, it might look like the one shown in Figure 3-2.

This "roadmap"—complete with escape routes—might appear complex at first glance, but if you go through it step by step, it's as logical and as simple as it can be!

In support of this escape route technique, it's a good idea to have a wealth of facts at your finger tips that will overwhelm a particular objection when it arises. Keep this information in a backup data section, at your finger tips, while you are making calls. Backup data information is generated by the checklist questions covered earlier. This section should be developed to help overcome common objections and should be used when a prospect makes a major issue out of some problem.

A woman, involved in selling corporate aircraft, uses the backup data system to enormous advantage.

How Vera M. Uses Backup Facts to Get the Advantage in Almost Every Call

In selling jets at $1.5 to $2 million each, Vera M. runs into a vast spectrum of objections. She encounters everything from price resistance to prospect doubts about handling characteristics.

Because of the many different obstacles she must confront, Vera obviously can't preempt. Also, she finds the re-

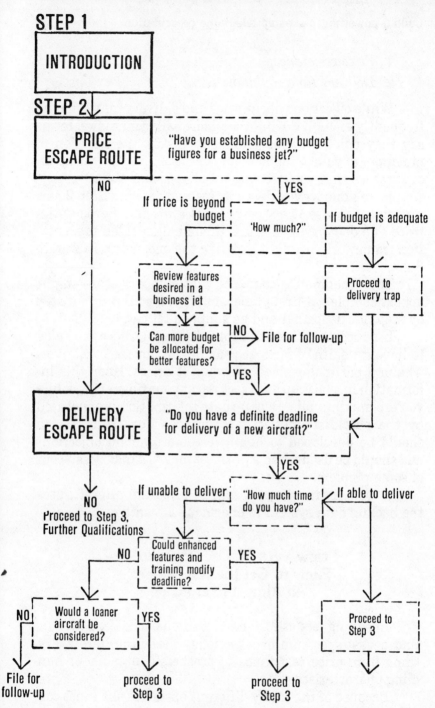

Figure 3-2

cently discussed technique of flushing out prominent objections highly impractical. She deals with these problems by having *strong factual rebuttals* ready when obstacles arise during her telephone presentations. Vera makes extensive use of a backup data section in her telephone presentation.

A few of the backup categories she has in front of her are as follows:

- Performance specifications
- Seating options
- Maintenance requirements
- Federal air regulations for commercial jet transports
- Instrumentation options
- Amortization schedules
- Safety record
- Resale history

Obviously, there isn't any way to incorporate these and other important categories into a relatively brief telephone presentation. But any of these topics could very well arise during a call, and when one does, Vera is ready to deliver authoritative facts that usually swing the discussion in her favor.

As soon as she has successfully knocked over objections, Vera proceeds without delay to Step 3, the *qualification phase* of her telephone presentation. Chapter 4 illustrates the building of an effective qualification question pattern.

zero in on the hot telephone prospects fast by qualifying them!

Bob V., a supplier of home alarm systems, rarely spends more than two or three minutes on a prospect who does not respond affirmatively to qualification questions asked during the initial telephone contact.

While Bob and his salespeople are friendly and polite, they are straightforward as well; no punches are pulled in their questioning, and no sidesteps are used in responding to the *prospect's* questions.

"Our totally 'open' approach creates immediate trust and credibility," says Bob. "The prospect gets a strong impression that no matter what kind of questions he asks, we'll come across with frank answers.

"We get to the point quickly . . . without the usual meaningless conversation many salespeople believe in. We know the person is busy, and we respect his time. He sees our concern, and his normal defenses go down. He relaxes and *wants* to tell us more and hear more about what we can do for him.

"Any intelligent prospect knows that *we're asking these qualification questions so we can determine if it makes sense to pursue the matter.* Why waste time giving a sales pitch if there's no reasonable basis for the person to use one of our alarm systems? He's as anxious to clear the air as we are."

This "up-front" approach works for Bob. It creates an ideal environment for the ultimate goal of the telephone presentation: A sale via phone, or an agreement for a field sales visit.

When Bob's salespeople qualify raw leads for possible field sales appointments, they begin their qualification series with general questions and proceed to more specific areas. Let's take a closer look at that technique.

The "Funnel" Principle in Qualifying Inquiries

The highest earning salespeople are not necessarily those who possess an extraordinary ability to persuade others. More often, they are people who are adept at zeroing in on the real buyers by asking *qualification questions.*

By separating the genuine prospects from the "tire-kickers," a smart salesperson spends the shortest time possible piling up impressive profits.

The only practical way to distill the relatively few high-probability inquiries from a large number of advertising or direct mail responses is through *qualifying.* This screening process is also the only feasible way to pinpoint the *real buyers* if you call from a cold list, as Bob V.'s people often do in selling alarm systems.

> *Screening is a carefully constructed series of questions intended to classify your prospect in terms of readiness-to-buy.*

As Figure 4-1 demonstrates, the Step 3 screening (or qualification) pattern starts with a broad qualifying question that eliminates the most obviously *unqualified* prospects. It then progresses to more specific questions designed to identify the people you have the best chance of closing now or in the very near future.

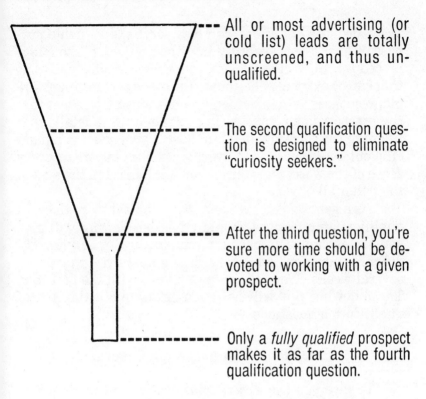

All or most advertising (or cold list) leads are totally unscreened, and thus unqualified.

The second qualification question is designed to eliminate "curiosity seekers."

After the third question, you're sure more time should be devoted to working with a given prospect.

Only a *fully qualified* prospect makes it as far as the fourth qualification question.

Figure 4-1

As you will see in a moment, the qualification procedure that turns out to be right for you may differ from the examples in this book. But, the *pattern* should simplify creation of one that will work very effectively for you.

How Much Qualifying Is Necessary?

Unless you are trying to close a sale during the initial phone call, it's possible to qualify most prospects right out of the ballpark! If the purpose of your call is to set up a strong field sales visit, *you simply want to assure that any further time you spend on this potential customer is apt to be fruitful.* Nothing more!

Adequate qualifying can also serve the valuable purpose of giving you visibility into the prospect's "shopping" procedure. Such insight lets you make recommendations that can be extremely helpful to the other person. For example, responses to your screening questions may reveal that the prospect is not considering certain crucial details that relate to the contemplated purchase. By suggesting a more efficient selection process, you become an expert in every sense of the word, and your value is enhanced in the eyes of the potential buyer.

As a general rule, at least three and not more than six qualification questions should be asked. *Testing* will give you the optimum number for your product or service. Try different questions, and vary the number over a period of several weeks. Track the results and go with the best mix. The following tips will help you set up a starting list of qualification questions.

Establishing Qualification Criteria

To give you the sort of qualification information you want, your screening questions should be devised on a scientific basis. *They should provide a picture of where your prospect stands in certain areas.* Let's look at some critically important areas that may apply to your product or service:

1. *Is the person you are talking to a decision maker?* This is always question number one, since you can't make headway dealing with a person of no authority.

2. *Have the applications for your product or service been established?* This is a general question and should be asked early in the qualification procedure. An answer like, "We're just thinking about different uses," could mean there is no real interest or that a decision is in the future. In any event, this area ascertains the overall time frame you have to deal with.

3. *Does the prospect have a particular price category in*

mind? Price consideration can tell a lot about how far your prospect's thinking has developed. If budget has entered into the shopping procedure, it sometimes indicates good buying potential.

4. *If applicable, have financing plans been investigated?* As with price, if the financing question is being contemplated, you could have yourself a good close possibility.

5. *Are any other sources of supply being considered?* The answer you get might provide a good clue as to the seriousness of the inquiry. Also, you may learn something about how stiff your competition is likely to be, and which features you should stress to neutralize those rivals.

Each of these facets should be explored during screening, plus others you develop as you build your own presentation. You may want to probe some more deeply than others, but each helps to provide a meaningful total profile of your prospect. Only then can you comfortably proceed with the next steps in the telephone-selling process.

The eye-opening case that follows dramatically points out how diligent qualifying bagged a sale of nearly $1 million that would have been missed under typical circumstances.

A Junkyard Visit Nets Lloyd C. $73,000 in Commissions

Lloyd C., the Sales Manager of a plastic injection molding plant, described a situation with which he was personally involved only a year earlier. A direct mail inquiry that had been assigned to one of Lloyd's representatives was rejected by that person. The card turned up on the Manager's desk marked "No Good." When Lloyd asked the salesperson the reason for the rebuff, he got a patient explanation about how the company was a small garbage collection firm—one of many in the city, with no apparent applications for complex plastic parts such as the firm produced. In addition, the lead came from a "bad neighborhood," one the salesperson had no desire to visit.

Lloyd saw a bit of logic in the appraisal, so did not make an issue of the arbitrary judgment of his employee. But, later that day, he called the company himself.

The person who answered the phone turned out to be the owner of the refuse collection company. Not an encouraging start in Lloyd's view. The next qualification question disclosed that a valid application did exist. The owner was developing a revolutionary new garbage pickup system that required precision molded parts. It was beginning to get interesting.

Through his next qualifying question, Lloyd discovered that financing was more than adequate, rendering insignificant the fact that this small company maintained headquarters in a dreary hole-in-the-wall. In fact, the firm was pondering three competing offers for rights to the new system, pending final development.

Lloyd drove out there the same day and easily set up a purchase that would ultimately total just over $1 million—and pay the Manager $73,000 in commissions over a three-year span!

After that, the plastics firm made it a policy that *every* inquiry would be personally contacted by telephone and thoroughly qualified, whether it appeared promising or not on the surface.

Making Qualification Questions
Conversational and Natural

An ever-present danger of using prearranged qualification questions is that they come out sounding "canned." Take care to weave the questioning process into your normal conversational style. The benefits are well worth the effort.

Since it is exceedingly difficult to "listen to yourself" as you are delivering the questions, try practicing on an associate or family member—or use a tape recorder to evaluate your naturalness.

One valuable tip is to *slow down*. Most people tend to repeat a planned delivery at an accelerated rate. Fast speech comes across as high-pressured. Also, be conscious of voice volume; make a concerted effort to speak more softly during a presentation.

Some of the most effective telephone salespeople are so low key that they actually sound tranquilized! Perhaps that is a bit extreme, but the point is this: Your prospect will often fall into the same mood that *you* are projecting. If there is anxiety in your voice, you'll get anxiety back from the other person. If you sound relaxed, your potential customers will tend to relax.

While you are thinking about being natural, give some thought to what your prospect is saying.

Evaluating Responses to Categorize Your Prospect Accurately

Many people listen but don't hear. When screening and qualifying, you have to *hear,* then accurately assess your prospect's position. Solid analysis can be tricky if a prospect's responses are nebulous. Here's an example:

You: "Have you worked out the specific applications for a precision lathe?"

Prospect: "Just some basic ones."

Does that response mean a decision is off in the future, or that various applications are now being considered and will soon be resolved? You can discover the answer only by probing further. Too many salespeople are intimidated by vague answers; they tend to regard them as put-offs. A little *clarification* will often turn a misty response into a crystal-clear qualification. Another type of response is frequently misinterpreted:

You:	"Do you have any particular price category in mind for a lathe?"
Prospect:	"We're not even close to that point. First, we have to clear up literally hundreds of other details in our company."

Is your contact saying that internal problems will indefinitely delay a decision, or that your help is needed in consultation? The above response might be a *buying* signal. You have to pursue the point to find out. Perhaps this way:

You:	"If those details relate to lathe specifications, we might be able to save you lots of time. We've installed scores of machines for companies in your industry, and we have a few facts you should know."

Try not to make assumptions based on borderline prospect responses. *Probe a little . . . it pays off!*

Pegging the Value of Your Prospect

When you have completed your screening questions, immediately proceed to categorize the prospect. Remember, the purpose of asking qualification questions is to arrive at an evaluation that will dictate your strategy; should you drop the inquiry as hopeless, go for an immediate close, or try for some other appropriate disposition? Whatever your decision, it has to be made *quickly.* Your judgment has to be formulated *within the space of a few seconds*—just before you jump from the qualification questions to the next step in your telephone presentation.

To act that rapidly, you have to set up clear categories. And your prospect's qualification answers have to point *directly* to one of those concisely defined slots.

There are typical categories you can use as a model.

Setting Up Categories from "Hot" to "Cold"

If you sell a product or service that can be closed via telephone, on the initial contact, this system might not apply. But, if you are qualifying for further follow-up, categorizing is *essential!*

Your system can be as simple and as straightforward as this:

Class "A" Prospect . . Can be closed on the next step of the sale (eg. an order, appointment, demo of the product etc.) now or within a few weeks.

Class "B" Prospect . . Very good, but will probably need more work such as sending literature and calling back. Determine the problem area, and concentrate on resolving it.

Class "C" Prospect . . Good possibility for the future. Perhaps various developments have to take place in your prospect's business first. Follow up in 30 days, or after appropriate wait.

Class "D" Prospect . . Needs are not well developed, and the situation is beyond your control. Contact again in six months.

Class "E" Prospect . . Not a potential buyer at this time. Don't spend any more of your valuable time.

Five categories can usually cover all degrees of prospect interest from "Hot" (A) to "Cold" (E). A good percentage of "C" and "D" prospects can eventually develop into an "A" or "B"—but whatever you do, don't dwell on "E's"! Your time is too valuable.

In categorizing prospects, your goal is to remove as much of the "gut level" feeling from the appraisal process as you can. Your contact might be (and probably is) an agreeable and friendly individual. But that should *not* influence your judgment of readiness-to-buy! Peg the prospect *strictly* on the answers you get to your qualification questions.

The main purpose of assigning an "A" to "E" rating to each contact is to *establish a follow-up priority system.*

What a Priority System
Can Do for You

Having every lead in a specific category saves you enormous time, as the following scenario suggests.

On Monday, you receive two calls from local companies asking about your product. In addition, you get 12 direct mail responses, plus a referral from a prior customer.

By day's end, you have contacted all 15 leads by telephone and have set field appointments with 10 of them over the next two weeks. On Tuesday, you get eight more inquiries and make six appointments. But a few "A"-rated leads that sound promising have to be delayed two weeks because of your growing workload. Wednesday brings more of the same—and on it goes.

Prioritizing almost completely eliminates the problem of not getting to the "A" prospects first. Reserving your earliest free time for the companies that qualify most strongly is the foundation of sales success. You work smarter, not harder.

Your objectives in seeing the highest priority ("A" and "B" rated) people first are:

1. To make the most income you can in the shortest possible time.

2. To get the order before your competition has a chance to react.

3. To set a comfortable pace for yourself.

We'll cover follow-up in more detail later.

Turning Marginal Prospect
Qualifications Into Tangible Needs

During slow business periods or when leads are sparse, you may decide to ease up a bit on your qualification requirements. When sales are flying, you may out of necessity turn your back on a prospect who hasn't decided on specific applications for your product. But when every lead counts, you're more inclined to work on cultivating this person.

Let's take that general application question, and explore the various directions it can take you:

You: "Do you have definite applications in mind for a computer?"

Prospect: "I haven't had time to work out specific uses yet, but we might be able to justify a purchase in six months or so."

If you have an appointment schedule packed with "A" rated prospects, this lead becomes a "D" or maybe a "C" if you stretch it. But if you have a quota to meet—and no abundance of business—you are more apt to perceive glimmers of hope, faint as they may be.

In the above case, you *continue* your qualification series just as if the prospect's answers had been:

"Yes! I have ten applications just waiting for your computer!"

Thus, if responses to your remaining questions are at least neutral, go for a field sales appointment that offers a chance for an order.

The following section tells of a young woman selling word-processing systems, who has developed her own very effective method of qualifying prospects.

How Van D. Converts Difficult Leads
Into Big Buyers Through
an Ingenious System of Qualifying

Van usually follows a predetermined pattern of qualification questions. But occasionally she encounters a prospect who will not go along with answering her. She has determined that some people resist for no logical reason. For a long time, Van threw her hands up in despair when she ran into this unexplained reluctance. Her practice was to cut the call short and move on to the next inquiry. She reasoned that if a person refused to communicate, there would be practically no chance of ending up with a sale.

Then, strictly by accident, Van discovered how wrong she had always been. One day a prospect gave her absolutely no worthwhile response to the most basic qualification questions. This time, instead of getting off the line, Van said, "If you could have *any* features you wanted in a word processor—*with no limitations at all*—how would you describe it, and what functions would it perform in your business?"

There was a pause on the other end, and Van could sense the wheels turning. Finally, the answer came in a torrent! By throwing the entire matter open as she did, the saleswoman had turned a magic key that demolished the prospect's reservations. In a four-minute statement, the prospect answered every unasked qualification question—plus a few!

As a rule, it's more effective to *control* the screening process. But now and then Van's strategy can work magic.

Let's proceed to the next step in the presentation: the building of a powerful product description.

putting a ton of punch into your telephone power-selling program

5

When a prospect "survives" your series of qualification questions, it is assumed that this basic point has been settled: The person or company you called meets all your standards and is definitely a buying candidate.

That being the case, you go immediately to the next step in your presentation: the *description and trial close.*

Remember, at the completion of the qualification questions, your prospect still doesn't know much about your product or service and at this point might be getting extremely curious about it—if not downright anxious. It's *your* turn to talk and to impart the information that person is patiently waiting for.

The Product Presentation: Three Minutes or Less of Pure Selling Impact

It's very easy to get carried away and to launch into a ten-minute dissertation that covers every detail of your product. Unfortunately, that approach would bore most prospects stiff and keep them on the phone for too long. Use the following guidelines; they work!

If you have the sort of product or service that can be closed during the initial telephone contact . . . you do have to go into reasonable product detail before a close should be attempted. But your objective, in most cases, should be to deliver sufficient information in about three minutes.

If the purpose of your call is to qualify a prospect for a field sales appointment . . . you can really streamline your product description. It can often be delivered in two minutes or less. Most of the heavy information will be imparted when the face-to-face meeting takes place; the last thing you want to do is go into extensive detail during that first qualifying phone call.

With that rather drastic economy of words, what you *do* say must be good.

The Essential Rule of 100

You must capture your prospect's interest in the first 100 to 200 words of your presentation.

A listener's tolerance threshold is often extremely low, and you can't afford to abuse it. The "grabber" in Step 1 (described in Chapter 3) provides just enough of a hook to capture a tiny corner of the prospect's interest. But now, in the description, you have to positively rivet that potential buyer's attention.

Actually, you apply the same principles in the Step 4 product description as you did in the Step 1 "grabber." *Every* phrase is made to be as strong and as dramatic as you can make it. In creating the actual dialogue for your telephone presentation, it's really a case of using "grabbers" everywhere you can. All your language has to sparkle, be clear as crystal, and be grammatically correct. But the first 100 words are especially critical.

What exactly are "grabbers"? Here's an explanation.

"Grabbers" Load Your Sentences
with Sales Dynamite

Most telephone and field salespeople sound like they're reading from spec sheets when they try to build a strong case for their product. They somehow believe that prospects make decisions based on logic and dry data.

You've heard it a million times: You have to sell the sizzle, *not* the steak. That's just one more way of saying you have to sell to a person's *emotions,* including love, fear, greed, power, and every other trigger that makes us react down deep.

That's precisely what "grabbers" are: well-aimed darts that hit prospects where they are most vulnerable. Those dull product performance figures that put most buying candidates into a sound sleep make very few sales.

The strength of every word you say is particularly critical when your communication time is severely limited, as it is when you are using the telephone to close a sale or set a solid apointment for a field sales visit.

Let's get into the mechanics of building "grabbers."

An experienced technical products saleswoman uses this fascinating formula to assure that dull telephone language is kept to an absolute minimum in her various presentations.

The "Proofer's Progression":
How Lana K. Assures That
Every Word Is Packed with Sell

A *technically correct* product description is the first priority in the company Lana works for. Her prospects, Data Processing Managers, are a critical audience, and simply will not sit still for sloppy or incomplete descriptions when they're shopping for computer components.

Each of her product descriptions is meticulously developed—usually by members of the firm's engineering staff. Needless to say, the result is usually an accurate summary of facts . . . but deadly boring as only a technical manual can be.

At first, Lana actually used the colorless descriptions created by technicians. She got nowhere. The language turned off even *other* technicians. In her first try at brightening up the phrases, the saleswoman achieved little. The problem? She found it difficult to identify *ordinary* words that could be transformed into exciting words and perhaps even emotional triggers.

The breakthrough for Lana came from a friend who happened to be a professional proofreader. This person explained to the saleswoman that when text is read in the customary way—from beginning to end—it's the overall content that really comes through. Individual words just don't stand out. She told Lana that the way to really examine something word for word is to read the whole thing *backwards!* This progression forces the reader to appraise each word by itself, with no thought given to a sentence or a paragraph's meaning.

When Lana applied this technique to her product descriptions, the "dead" words popped out like sore thumbs. She was then able to replace them with *alive* language without compromising the technical correctness of the content.

The change brought swift results. The saleswoman's close ratio rose steeply.

The words Lana uses to strengthen her presentations are *not* magic. They are part of your daily vocabulary.

A Library of Action Words
That Make Sales

The boldface words evoke *far* more prospect response than their counterparts to the left.

effect	—	**impact**
versatile	—	**multi-faceted,**
		all-encompassing

interesting	—	**colorful, fascinating, riveting**
quiet	—	**soundless**
economical	—	**cost-effective**
up-to-date	—	**state-of-the-art**
complex	—	**elaborate, highly-detailed**
emergency	—	**crisis**
checkpoint	—	**benchmark**
capacity	—	**potential**
skill	—	**expertise, genius**
hopeful	—	**enthusiastic**
trim	—	**sleek**
surprise	—	**astonish**
good	—	**fantastic**
better	—	**superior**
energy	—	**force**
difficult	—	**formidable, tough**
produce	—	**generate**
popular	—	**renown, distinguished**
inflexible	—	**rigid**
dismal	—	**ominous**
unusual	—	**exotic, radical**

That's the general idea. There is usually a better way to describe something, especially when technical people provide the first draft. *Roget's Thesaurus* is a reference book that can supply scores of alternative words to choose from.

Critically look at *every* word in the first draft of your presentation. Use the "proofer's progression" to evaluate each one in terms of its selling power. Replace the weak words with ones that evoke more excitement.

The above list is just a sampling. Begin building your own library of power and action words, and *use* them in all selling situations.

Back to Lana K. for a moment. She uses the following tactic to involve her prospect in the product description.

Drawing Your Prospect Into
the Product Description:
How to Do It

A phrase in one of Lana's product presentations was written by technicians to concisely and properly describe one of the company's new systems:

> The Model T841 transmits data from remote locations to central computers. This system is designed for large firms with dispersed locations since its data compression feature doubles data transmission throughput which results in lower communication cost.

Factual? Yes. Dull? Decidedly. Any Data Processing Manager *would* understand that spoken paragraph, but few would get truly involved in it. So Lana did a little rearranging.

Through her qualification step, she'd know if a prospect transmitted data to a central computer from remote sites. She would use that bit of knowledge to *draw the prospect into the product presentation*. The result is a vast improvement over the original rendition. Here it is:

Lana: "You *do* have an extensive network of remote sites that transmit data to a central computer, right?"

Prospect: "That's correct."

Lana: "Would you be interested in reducing the high communication costs involved with dispersed sites?"

Prospect: "I'd certainly listen to what you have to say."

| Lana: | "Okay. Our T841 is *designed* for situations like yours. It *doubles* data transmission throughput with its data compression feature." |

Thus, a passive paragraph of descriptive dialogue can be easily changed into a powerful and convincing *two-way* conversation. It draws the prospect into inevitable conclusions. This is stronger by far than merely delivering the words to an uninvolved listener!

Here are two other professional tips for drawing people more deeply into your telephone sales scenario.

Pauline R.'s Twin-Edged Method for Getting Prospects Involved Through the Clever Use of Words

Pauline sells market research services to industrial companies. The greatest challenges facing her are convincing prospects and drawing them out via the telephone. Over the years, the telephone saleswoman has learned of many "tricks" designed to more fully persuade and involve prospects. She tested most of them at one time or another, and finally zeroed in on two that steadily bring her results.

The Yale 12

The Psychology Department at Yale University identified 12 words of extraordinary persuasive power. Pauline makes it a point to build each one into every telephone presentation she gives because her own meticulous testing indicated that they do, indeed, work. Here they are:

- you
- money
- save
- new
- easy
- discovery
- results
- proven
- guarantee
- free
- love
- help

Whenever possible, Pauline combines as many as four of these convincing buzzwords in one super-persuasive sentence!

The "playback"

Asking questions of her prospects can be frustrating for Pauline. Very often she receives one-word answers, which often don't get her very far. The "playback" lets her gently draw out even the most reticent prospect. The "playback" *consists of repeating the last several words of the prospect's last sentence, and putting a question mark after them.* An example follows:

> Prospect: "We're looking into some areas that might reveal a need for special data."
>
> You: "Special data?"
>
> Prospect: "Yes . . . such as information about our competitors, product applications, and maybe potential new markets."
>
> You: "New markets?"

And so forth. The "playback" is a gentle, probing technique that digs out ever-deepening layers of information. It gives you an ideal tool for getting prospects involved.

While you're busy sharpening your word skills, it's a good idea to be thinking about product or service features you can dramatize. The following guidelines should help you.

In Search of Facts You Can Dramatize

You sit down to begin work on writing your product description. Spread out before you are product brochures, notes you took when you went through the checklist questions (Chapter 3) with product experts, and other factual material you have gathered. Now, where do you begin? You possess so *much* data that the problem becomes a question of what to eliminate!

The best clue, of course, is the feedback you received when you asked the checklist question about the most important customer benefits associated with your product or service. If you didn't have the advantage of an expert to consult with, the task of selecting winning product features is all yours.

If you do face the job of picking the most riveting topics, put yourself in the shoes of your typical customer. A very good way to accomplish that is to interview a few customers to find out just how they perceive your goods. After all, they use whatever it is you sell, and there is nobody who is better qualified to list the strongest benefits in order of importance.

Talk to several customers to get a balanced point of view. When you conduct these impromptu interviews, try not to influence their thinking by bringing up various features. Throw the discussion wide open, for example, by asking, "What do you like most about our widgets?"

Take the few most outstanding benefits and build them into a description for Step 4 of your presentation. Then put the advantages of *secondary* importance into your backup data as supporting information, to be used as needed to achieve your telephone call objectives.

A truck parts salesman uses the following system for developing solid but brief descriptions.

Ken T.'s "Triangle Principle" Builds Hard-Hitting Messages

During 12 years of selling replacement truck parts, Ken T. tried every conceivable product pitch in his telephone work.

He went from elaborate reports on part durability to pitches on safety and economy. The results never varied significantly despite wild swings in emphasis.

Ken knew he had to provide at least basic data about an axle assembly or an oil cooler, but the correct balance and format never really felt right, and certainly weren't setting the world on fire as far as closes were concerned. Then, years later, he discovered the "triangle principle" quite accidentally.

While doodling one day during a lengthy phone call to a prospect, Ken absently listed the *main* topic of conversation that had taken place only moments before. Around that topic heading, he added one-word descriptions of other ideas the two men had been discussing.

Finally, without conscious motivation, Ken connected the words with a line. The call finally ended. An $11,000 order had been finalized. After he finished writing the order, Ken glanced at his sheet of random sketches and saw this:

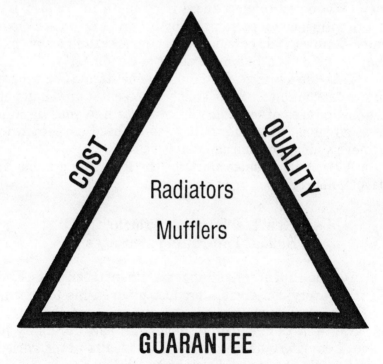

Figure 5-1

It struck him that this big order had been made by verbally "packaging" every parts product in a three-fact argument consisting of cost, quality, and guarantee of performance. Ken suddenly realized that no matter *what* kind of truck part he tried to sell, those three elements had to be built into the description.

It works like this. A brief rundown of details about radiators, mufflers, or any other part is followed by price information. The cost statement is immediately justified through a sentence or two about quality. The company's guarantee policy is last; it adds that final measure of reassurance.

The vital elements in *your* recipe may differ from Ken's, but there *is* a formula that will win consistently for you.

Three Ways to Guarantee
Impact on Your Prospect

Even the best combination of topics for your product description will fail unless it is *understood*. These three guidelines help assure optimum prospect comprehension.

- **Go for Clarity**

    Keep language simple. Plain talk won't provide a showcase for your extensive vocabulary, but the points you have to make will get across in no uncertain terms. Complex sentences and fancy words tend to stop otherwise rapt listeners; they dwell on something that was said while the speaker rambles on.

    A little later, you'll find a formula that guarantees the creation of understandable language.

- **Create Vivid Mental Images**

    Help your prospect *visualize*. When children pretend, they *are* visualizing effectively. This is particularly valuable in telephone selling since you don't have the benefit of graphic aids. You create mental images by *asking* the prospect to imagine. For example:

"What would happen if one of your work crews was up at the 40th floor on a scaffold, and gale-force winds suddenly came up? It could be a *disaster* without our Tuffy Stabilization System!"

This approach is infinitely more descriptive and colorful than a flat explanation. The prospect's imagination will do its *own* selling job.

- **Talk to a Person**

Too many telephone marketers forget there's a *person* on the other end of the line. The process of calling becomes impersonal. You have to frequently remind yourself about the other human being to keep from losing that vital warmth.

Your inner feeling about that other person will be conveyed in your voice. No act can conceal a caller's lack of empathy.

How Bill D.'s Clarity Evaluation System Assures Perfect Communications

Bill's eyes were opened rather rudely one day as he was telephoning prospects. One prospect expressed immediate interest in the office furniture rental package the salesman was offering. But when Bill finished delivering his description—actually the *essence* of his message—the prospect remained mysteriously silent.

Bill asked the prospect for a reaction, and received this statement: "Pardon me, but I understood everything you said until you got into the details of how your deal works. At that point, you lost me completely."

It was a rude awakening. That same evening, the rental salesman started doing things differently. Bill began using what he now calls his "Clarity Evaluation System." This, he felt, would *guarantee* perfect communications with every potential buyer. It's a two-phase program that works this way: Months earlier, Bill learned of a formula called *The Fog Index and Readability Yardstick, developed by the Gunning-Mueller Clear Writing Institute* in Santa Barbara, California. The Index is easy to use.

First, Bill takes a passage he has written for his description. He then calculates the average number of words for each sentence in that passage. Next, the salesman counts the words in each 100-word passage that have three syllables or more. Bill then adds the two figures, and multiplies by 0.4. The total equals the number of years of education (up to 17) a reader would need to understand the description! For example, this paragraph, and the one preceding it, would work out this way:

> 14 words in the average sentence
> 10 words of three syllables or more in each 100
> ____ words
>
> 24
> × 0.4
> ____
> 9.6 years of education needed to understand the above two paragraphs

The second phase of Bill's Clarity Evaluation System consists of a live test. He has found that, by aiming for *eight to ten years of education* in his Readability Yardstick, there will be *maximum comprehension* of his presentation.

Bill has a nephew and niece at an educational level that qualify them to participate in a trial run. He calls them individually and delivers the script. Then he asks for a brief report on the details of what he said. Only if each youngster can repeat the major points is the salesman convinced that his words are properly selected.

For language that is easily understood, most telephone professionals aim for the education mark of eight to ten years. The truth is, even more highly educated listeners appreciate uncomplicated language.

Three Ways to Create Mental Images
That Help Make Drab Products Irresistible

Avoid at all costs using the kind of language commonly found in annual reports. A reader finds many of them dull, and a listener doesn't come off much better.

Your objective is to create colorful, compelling language for telephone presentation descriptions. This thrusts the prospect into a situation where he or she actually *experiences* use of a product or a service. You create a scenario with words, and it provokes vivid mental images.

These three easy-to-use guidelines go a long way toward helping you to accomplish this goal:

• The way you *preface* a phrase makes a difference, using lead-ins like . . .

> "What if *you* were president of the corporation, and had our monthly reports to help you run six divisions. . . ."

> or:

> "Picture yourself slipping behind the wheel and handling this coupe at high speed on a winding mountain road. . . ."

> Better language by far than, "It has excellent road-holding characteristics thanks to independent front suspension!"

• Try to stay away from "to be" words such as *would, could, will, can,* and the like. Instead, put your prospect solidly in the present. Use *is, does* and *are* to give your listener a strong sense of the present moment. This powerfully supports the tactic of putting the person into an action situation that can be clearly visualized.

• This is *extremely* important: **Write your presentation as closely as possible to the way you talk.** Most people become much more formal when they write compared to the way they speak. You are apt to say:

"We're the biggest supplier of insulated pipe in the midwest, so you're sure to get quick delivery of needed sizes just by picking up the phone."

But you might be apt to *write:*

"We are the major warehouser of insulated pipe in the central states. Therefore, yóu are certain to receive prompt delivery of most specified sizes when you contact our order department."

If your script is overly formal, your natural speech flow may tend to become stiff. *Write it the way you want to talk it.* A tape recorder can help tremendously.

You can weave the following important tactic into the overall fabric of your telephone description to create a more favorable closing environment.

Carla V.'s "Yes-Response" Gets Automatic Closes

Sales are made in small steps. It's like a trial lawyer who wins seemingly insignificant points during the proceedings, but has successfully built them into a major case by the end of the contest.

Obvious as that concept may seem, it hit Carla very hard one day when she was running into resistance at the close stage of her telephone presentation. Selling major home improvements took every bit of punch she could muster, and something was definitely lacking.

She did draw prospects into the picture by describing increased comfort, enhanced property value, and prestige. But when the close came, Carla found herself offering a giant "yes" or "no" option, and the "no" was winning.

Like a trial attorney, the saleswoman decided to attain her objective through success in a series of small engagements. Throughout her description, Carla placed a number of questions she was *certain* would evoke affirmative responses from the prospect. For example, after explaining how a covered patio would increase the coziness and intimacy of a backyard, Carla added: "Would you be more likely to *use* a patio designed like that?"

A string of agreements from a prospect created a *"Yes"* response. Carla noticed that this affirmative reaction *did* bring about a higher likelihood that the final prospect answer would also be a "Yes!"

That thoroughly covers the planning, structuring, and writing of a winning power-selling telephone presentation. Now, let's carefully explore the methods developed and used by some of America's top earners.

inside technique tips from America's leading telephone money-makers

6

An athlete will study the attributes of other outstanding performers on the field of play. By observing the techniques of those considered to be masters of the sport, the observing competitor can sharpen his or her own skills. This is a strongly recommended way of promoting self-improvement, but there is an element of danger in it.

Evaluating the style and moves of another can modify the way a watcher performs naturally. This process may begin harmlessly enough, but it can gradually introduce changes in timing, stance, and even general attitude. In other words, getting pointers is okay, but *copying* can really send you into a deep slump.

Be You . . . Don't Attempt to Imitate Someone Else!

You possess inherent and unique strengths. It makes good sense to cultivate those personal attributes, then apply them in areas where they will do you the most good. One salesperson may be incomparable in dealing with irate customers. Another might be unsurpassed in dealing with top-level executives, and so forth. For each "type," there's a field of endeavor that fits ideally.

In the process of absorbing this book, it is expected that you will respond more strongly to certain parts, and less to others. Whatever you do, use *only* the tactics and techniques that feel right. When you find yourself admiring the techniques of someone you work with or observe in some other circumstances, keep it in perspective and don't imitate!

Your *rate of delivery and cadence* are distinct trademarks of your personal style and can be developed to make you much stronger on the telephone.

Manipulating Your Speaking Rhythm for Better Listener Response

The best impersonators study the *rhythm* of a voice they are trying to master because it's as distinctive as the beat in a musical score. Although they are important factors, it is not necessarily the pitch of the voice or a person's vocabulary that makes a certain speaker more "listenable" than another.

Your natural rhythm is essentially a built-in *characteristic*. It would be a major task to permanently change it, and probably a pointless undertaking in view of our earlier advice to make the most of your inherent qualities. But you can and should teach yourself to *vary* your rhythm when you want to emphasize a prominent point.

For example, your tempo should quicken when a particularly momentous parcel of information is to be delivered. Your cadence should be slower than normal when an especially complex passage comes up.

Many telephone salespeople believe they vary their rhythm, but in fact, they are merely increasing or decreasing the volume of their voice! Here again, a tape recording will provide a positive means of developing that skill.

An extremely successful attorney, known for his extraordinary speech before juries, has another very good way of changing tempo to fit the occasion.

Felix P. Discovers That
Body Articulation Enhances Voice Appeal

Felix was losing more than his share of cases because his voice was flat, uninteresting, and unconvincing. As a trial lawyer, one of his most important tools was the quality of his voice. The problem beset him not only in the courtroom situations, but in the many functions he had to accomplish by telephone as well.

The attorney was determined to exercise will power and introduce "life" into his voice, but the myriad details of a case invariably broke that concentration, and he reverted back to a drab monotone. He simply didn't have time to practice in the little spare time available, so the problem seemed hopeless.

The trial lawyer had all but resigned himself to the shortcoming when a legal secretary put a newspaper article on his desk about effective public speaking. The part that really made sense to Felix was this:

> *The writer, a respected speech therapist, maintained that voice modulation, tempo, and overall drama are enhanced when a speaker is physically animated. When hands, arms, and body are immobilized during speech, the voice reflects that absence of motion.*

Felix immediately began using his body when talking. In court, he drove home a strong point by a fist into his opened hand; he dramatized an elaborate description by two hands raised in the same manner a maestro conducted a symphony; he illustrated a threatening mood by feet planted firmly on the floor, hands on hips.

The instant improvement in *live* situations prompted

Felix to apply the same techniques to *his telephone work*. If the impact of his speech had been so vastly increased in face-to-face encounters, why wouldn't *his telephone voice* undergo the very same transformation?

At first Felix felt ridiculous sitting alone in his office on a call, waving and pointing his hands as if someone were seated before him. But the *power* Felix knew he was gaining overcame that initial awkwardness. It worked so well, he had a speaker phone installed, and now he paces around his desk during a phone call just as if he was pleading to a jury!

Animation to strengthen your telephone-power can be taken yet another step further. Let's look at the way it's done.

Two Ways to Project Your Personality

Outstanding radio broadcasters are known to "project." The emotion they generate reaches out to the listener as surely as it would if they were in the same room viewing the event as it unfolded.

Projecting can be nicely accomplished by reacting spontaneously. When a game-winning, grand slam home run is hit, the sports broadcaster shouts gleefully along with the thunderous eruption from the stadium grandstands. A factual statement of events, related in a matter-of-fact tone of voice, would soon create discontent among radio listeners.

That's the extreme. You are not likely to shout, stomp, and cheer to your prospect. But you certainly *can* display glee, amazement, shock, disappointment, and other emotions with your voice. True, your reactions *do* have to be somewhat modified when you talk to prospects, but you can certainly convey various moods clearly just the same.

Working with a structured telephone presentation format should *not* deprive you of free expression. Projecting your personality this way can be done *within* the prescribed steps. Relax, and don't hesitate to make the conversation exciting for the person on the other end of the line!

And don't forget to *visualize your prospect*. Although you have probably never met the individual you're calling, try to build a mental image of what he or she looks like, and what his or her immediate environment is.

When you visualize, you are effectively focusing on the other person instead of staring absently at a stapler, doodling on a pad, or other distracting motions. The building of a mental image strongly projects your personality and brings life and animation to your telephone work.

While you're practicing these remarkably effective techniques, remember overall business demeanor.

Professionalism Opens Doors

Conveying an image of professionalism will uncover opportunities for you that ordinary salespeople miss. The fact is, certain buyers are extremely discerning about whom they do business with, and simply will not "open the door" to those who are less than dignified.

Dignity *can* be maintained at the same time you express enthusiasm. One really has no connection with the other. Professionalism can be defined as *conducting your enterprise with complete respect for the feelings of your prospect or customer*. That includes having a generous measure of real concern for that person and his or her problems.

The following three guidelines can keep you on the track:

- "Loosen up" at the same rate your prospect does. For example, if you prefer to address people more formally as "Mr." Smith or "Mrs." Jones when a relationship is just beginning, it's usually wise to go on a first-name basis only after the prospect makes an initial move in that direction, or *asks* you to use first names.

- As a rule, bringing personal matters up in a new business relationship can bend it out of shape. The prospect may very well seem amused that your cat ate the price lists, but you can be certain that your image has tarnished.

- Anyone who is ever sold knows that "knocking" competitors is taboo. It may get your point across, but it almost always wrecks *your* image at the same time. Blasting rivals is unprofessional.

A fourth tip on protecting your business dignity is important enough to warrant more explanation.

Avoiding the Inappropriate and Cutting Out Clichés

A well-known telephone sales consultant described how one of his new callers wanted to approach a project:

"I hired this man to do the calling on a project for a major midwest company. We'd be contacting financial vice presidents. Because he was experienced, I asked him to come up with some suggestions for the presentation.

"The next day, he hands me a sheet with 15 or 20 ribald jokes written on it. I asked him what they were for, and he says they're to use in the calls—to 'warm-up' the prospects! *That* idea we didn't use . . . and I taught him a few things about appropriateness right then and there!"

Nearly any manager who has the responsibility of monitoring the dialogue of telephone callers runs into this phenomenon from time to time. Phrases of bad taste creep into the language, and results suffer. One recent example went like this: A caller for a high-technology firm wanted to stress the engineering prowess of the company and the large number of people on their technical staff. Somehow, her description took on the following negative slant:

". . . we allocate a higher-than-usual budget for research and development. In fact, our engineering department is *top-heavy*."

Watching the words and phrases you use in a telephone presentation is one thing, and weeding out clichés is another.

A seemingly innocent expression in one's language can come close to driving a listener to the verge of utter distraction. Here are a few cases in point:

- One caller punctuates almost every prospect statement with "I see."
- Another uses "Uh huh."
- Yet another follows on the heels of a prospect remark with *"really?"*

There are countless speech habits like these. Each one, when frequently repeated during the course of a presentation (and they always are used to excess), gradually irritates the listener.

The difficult thing about controlling this problem is that *most people aren't aware they do it!* It's far simpler to detect this quirk in the speech of others. Here again, a recording of your end of a presentation will reveal such bad habits; the clichés will pop out at you.

One more solid telephone sales practice is directly linked to professionalism. Let's explore it.

Total Candor Makes Sales and Bluffing Blows 'Em

Credibility is an absolutely necessary ingredient to success in selling by telephone. It is also an extremely delicate component. It takes a long time to build, but can be demolished in an instant. Candor is the main building block in credibility. Bluffing is the poison that kills it. The following is a situation you've undoubtedly seen.

You're on the phone with a prospect. Your commission stands to run thousands of dollars, and the prospect turns out to be fully qualified and very, very interested. The problem is, delivery is needed in two weeks, and you *know* it will take four weeks minimum.

Coming right out and saying you can't make the two-week deadline could very well blow this order away for good. You *might* tell the prospect that two weeks is no problem, then stall as long as you have to beyond that point. The deal might be canceled, but at least you'd have a shot at it.

Good business, of course, is coming right out with the truth, painful as it may be. *How that truth is explained,* however, is of the utmost importance. You wouldn't just say, "Sorry, we can't help you. Maybe next time." Better to say it this way:

> "There's nothing I'd like better than doing business with you, but I have a problem. The only way I'll operate is to be totally frank in every way—and I have to tell you that delivery will run about four weeks."

If the prospect has any sophistication at all, he or she will be aware that you *could have* bluffed (as all too many salespeople would). And, unless delivery is *really* a critical issue, that person will do everything within reason to see that *you* get the business because they *know* they'll get future orders when you say they will! Such is the power of credibility.

Questions may be asked by prospects that put you on the spot:

- How long have you been in business?
- Who are your clients in my industry?
- How big is your staff?

Here again, come up with answers of meticulous truth *without hesitation.* You'll win more than you lose over the long haul!

Candor is a traveling companion of *sincerity,* as you'll see now.

How Claire L. Builds Sincerity
When She Doesn't Feel It

As an investment counselor for a prestigious financial firm, Claire must be honest with her clients in every detail of a transaction. Along with this candor, her strong suit is sincerity; people trust the woman because they sense that she is genuinely concerned and real.

But problems arise now and then. Occasionally, the counselor phones a prospect who, for one reason or another, she does not like. Claire reacts to this with hostility. As she tries to conceal her feelings, they are somehow transmitted through the telephone line and picked up by the potential investor. As you would expect, this destroys any chance of a deal.

There *are* people in her office who are endowed with extraordinary tolerance; they might not respect a client, but the smile and sweetness continue to flow. Claire simply could not function that way . . . until she invented a system for overcoming her almost too real reactions.

The investment saleswoman uses *visualization* to neu tralize her bad feelings about certain prospects. In all telephone contacts (by which most of her business is conducted), Claire, in her imagination, substitutes a good friend for the offensive prospect or customer. As a result, the animosity vanishes, and these usually strained relationships normalize for Claire.

In describing her success with visualization, Claire also supplied a few valuable pointers about *tuning in* to the prospect.

The Four-Point Formula:
How Pros Listen to Win the Order

Claire maintains that most of the people who work for the investment firm, but don't make it, are poor listeners. The majority are eminently well-qualified for the job, and all are of above-average intelligence. But their inability or unwillingness to get involved in another person's point of view proves to be a fatal flaw.

Is the problem with these people egotism? Impatience? Or is it a breakdown in one or more of these basic four components of good listening: *hearing, interpretation, evaluation and response?*

Unless a person puts *all four* of those components to work in telephone selling (and in *all* communications with others) listening will be faulty and basic understanding will not be achieved.

Like any acquired talent, professional listening does have to be learned and continually practiced. Merely keeping still while the other person talks is only the beginning of good listening. To practice, make a concerted effort to do *each* of these things *every time your prospect says something:*

1. **Hear** what the other person says. Concentrate on every word, and while you're doing that, let the *overall meaning* sink in.

2. **Interpret** the main thrust of your prospect's thought. Sometimes you have to "read between the lines" to come up with the real meaning of someone's words. Are you *positive* you understood what was just said to you?

3. **Evaluate** what was said in terms of what you are offering. Get to the very heart of what your prospect wants, what his or her anxieties and desires are. Evaluation is actually the link between what was said by the prospect—and what your deal is.

4. **Respond** in a manner appropriate to what you've discovered in the first three steps. Your response has to be relevant to the prospect's main point. An off-target response is nearly always the trademark of a poor listener.

Using these four listening steps can enhance your telephone selling power in other ways. You'll find them interesting and helpful.

The "Power Pause"—
A Proven Winner for Juan H.

Juan imports fine linens and sells them to department stores. Most of his selling is done by telephone, and he freely admits the difficulty he encountered before applying the four-point listening formula. He is now able to establish rapport with buyers, where before it had been next to impossible.

But the importer feels that his strategy for tuning in has produced a surprise byproduct that may very well equal his new listening power in importance. He describes the unexpected windfall this way:

"Before, I not only didn't listen properly, but I started talking the second a buyer ended a sentence. I couldn't tolerate silence. In fact, sometimes my first word cut into the other person's last word.

"When I started using the four-point listening concept, I was literally *forced* to pause between the Evaluation phase and the Response phase. Before I could make any sort of intelligent response, I had to stop a moment to evaluate what the person was saying.

"That tiny wait—usually just a few seconds—really helps me keep control. I think it convinces the buyer that I am digesting what she just said."

It is *absolutely true* that short silences are extremely effective in telephone selling. They *do* lend importance to the prospect's statement, and they *certainly* create more drama for the response that will be coming from you.

Juan calls these golden little periods of silence his "power pauses." Now, rather than causing him discomfort, they serve as formidable tactical tools in his telephone technique arsenal.

If you properly *evaluate* the words of your prospect before you respond, this power pause will occur *automatically* during your telephone sales calls!

And, if you make every effort to thoroughly comprehend what is on your prospect's mind, you'll accomplish yet one more goal in effective telephone selling.

Probing to Gain Vice-Like Control

If you do decide to enhance your listening ability through the four-point formula, be careful to get all the facts you need to arrive at an accurate evaluation. If necessary, probe more deeply to obtain total clarification. Be sure you have the entire picture *before* you respond!

You'll discover that when you dig into the *smaller* details, a much sharper view of your prospect's needs will take shape. And as this occurs, your control of the overall situation will increasingly tighten. Look at it this way:

> *When a new acquaintance takes exceptional interest in what you are saying, you tend to have tremendous respect for that person. It's not a case where someone is merely listening to you and absently nodding agreement; it's a gentle but steady*

probing by the individual designed to uncover all the available facts about you. Very flattering indeed.

We move now to telephone *strategies* that generate big income for some of America's top calling pros.

penetrating tough defenses to sell top-level decision makers by telephone

7

All the technique, structure, guile, and charm in the world will fail if you can't direct these forces to centers of influence. In fact, *inferior* presentations may even outperform polished ones if they effectively reach an audience of authority and ability to buy.

Getting to the source of buying approval can be a particularly vexing problem to telephone salespeople who function in the area of offering products or services to other businesses. In many instances, decision makers insulate themselves by installing "lines of defense," which may consist of secretaries, administrative assistants, or other employees.

Your call to such a company is first answered by an operator at a main switchboard. You ask this usually pleasant individual for the person you want and your call is buzzed into the proper extension, no questions asked. It's too early to celebrate this remarkable progress, however, because the barriers are still a step away.

Now, a different but equally polite voice answers and announces that you have reached "Mr. Larson's office." Following a path of faultless logic, you ask, "Is he in, please?" And you begin to sense that it won't be quite that simple.

Next, the pleasant voice might ask you, "May I tell him what your call is in regard to?" An all too *typical* caller reaction is a slightly panicky attempt to disguise the true purpose of the call. The sudden realization that this key person might yet elude the interview is sometimes enough to destroy a salesperson's composure.

If that's what happens, the situation rapidly deteriorates.

If the caller fails to handle events professionally, the screener will inevitably say one of these things:

- "Mr. Larson wouldn't be interested in that."
- "I'll tell him about it, and he'll call you back if he's interested."
- He's in a meeting now—is leaving for Europe this afternoon—and will be at our out-of-town branch for six months when he returns next October."

The point is, screeners are a *fact of life* in the day-to-day activities of any caller doing business with medium to large companies. Encounters with them do *not* have to be characterized by rejection or conflict. More often than not, the various assistants who shield the boss can be won over, and can actually become assets to the telephone salesperson.

This chapter describes some of the ways that is accomplished.

Getting Past Secretaries: An Angle That Consistently Works for Clint Y.

In calling major industrial firms to sell his market research services, Clint was getting stopped in his tracks a discouraging number of times. Invariably, screeners would block his access to the top-level executives who represented his prime audience.

When asked by these people what he wanted of the boss, Clint felt his usually high level of patience begin to crumble. He reasoned this way: How could an ordinary secretary comprehend the intricacies of a research project? And further, how could such a minimally qualified individual relate *his* story to the top person with enough clarity and impact to win a personal appointment?

Clint's response to the simple request for a description of his mission was an exasperated two-sentence outburst that was barely understandable even to an expert in his field. Clint, in effect, was telling the screener to get lost and put him through to the boss. The reaction was predictable; the man *rarely* achieved an audience with his desired contact. Not only that, but he was causing severe damage to many potentially helpful business relationships.

The landmark change in his basic approach came when Clint met one of these screeners at a social function. The woman was an administrative assistant in the marketing department of a large electronics firm. She impressed Clint with her grasp of general business subjects and with her positive reaction to his services.

Suddenly, those "lower-level" people he had treated with such disdain took on an entirely new look. Clint realized that he could build a relationship with most screeners, and the majority were more than equal to the task of understanding his business and then *relaying a concise message to the boss.*

Starting immediately, the researcher began investing a few extra minutes in each call. He gave each screener a detailed description of his service and described *why* the top person would very likely be interested in learning more about the benefits of his service.

The payoff was quick in coming. Calls converted to

appointments at a tripled rate. Equally important, the rapport Clint had built with the screeners helped his progress with higher-ups in the prospective company.

This out-front strategy proves *vastly* superior to the subterfuge, half-truths and other ploys frequently used by telephone callers to "tunnel under" the people assigned to spare the boss unnecessary phone calls. And the philosophy of treating the screener like an intelligent human being is *certainly* more constructive than automatically regarding all assistants as mindless robots!

Two More Valuable Ways to Contact Decision Makers

Clint's forthright pitch to assistants will work in a surprising number of cases. But what about those occasional sales call screeners who resolutely refuse to be budged? In these instances, it does require a little more guile on your part—but *not* the kind that breeds animosity:

- Try calling the company after 5 p.m. Most secretaries and assistants leave work about that hour and, with luck, your call will ring right through to your main contact in the company. When the boss picks up the phone, he or she is usually not prepared to resist your strong presentation, so your chances of success are greatly enhanced.

- When a screener tells you, "Mr. Smith isn't interested in your (product or service)," respond this way:
  "I respect what you say, but I'd appreciate it if Mr. Smith would tell me that *himself.*"

Quite often, your request will be accepted, and you'll have a chance to personally convince Smith. When you get that opportunity, use it wisely, as suggested now.

Customizing a Presentation
for Elusive Prospects

Here's the scenario: You finally manage to get on the line with a high-up individual, who does possess buying power and is apparently very busy. You've been calling this firm for weeks, and never succeeded in getting past the secretary until today. Now you're in contact with the boss; you have to make a snap judgment and select one of the following two options: Do you deliver a quick but full-blown, step-by-step presentation? Or do you convey just your most salient product points out of respect for your prospect's obviously hectic schedule?

Most experts opt for the latter choice. In this instance, deliver *a sharply condensed version of your presentation.* Supporting this decision is the fact that a harassed and preoccupied executive is very likely to have an extremely short attention span. If this person gets the feeling that a caller is taking advantage of a rarely granted audience, resentment may very well wreck any chance of progress toward a sale, no matter *how* well-structured your telephone presentation is!

One more consideration is this. If you give the busy higher-level manager deserved credit for being above-average as an intelligent and perceptive judge, you'll realize that your shortened presentation will very probably impart enough information. He or she is *accustomed* to making decisions based on sparse but solid data.

Any adept seller of executives understands the need to tailor a presentation for a rushed listener. The only danger is if you start delivering *all* presentations in this cut-down mode! Stick to your step-by-step structure *unless you see clear indications that your prospect has strictly limited time to give you.*

Your abbreviated presentation can be as condensed as this:

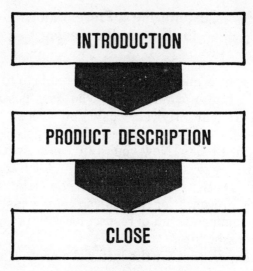

Figure 7-1

The "grabber" can be dropped from the Introduction since you'll jump directly into the Product Description, without the intervening qualification step. When dealing with this type of hard-to-catch prospect, you have to move swiftly and strongly to a successful outcome.

Walt M.'s Power-Closes
for Hitting "Moving Targets"

While the brief presentation deprives you of the all-important qualification stage, and doesn't allow enough time for certain other helpful telephone sales tactics, it *does* permit you to be especially bold in the close.

Walt M. offers a high-ticket but important management development course. He estimates that well over half of his telephone calls encounter tough screening. Through persistence, he eventually reaches his contact about 70 percent of the time—but not before he is told he has only "a minute" or "a few seconds" to complete his message.

In some cases, Walt senses that the warning to hurry is more a routine request than a genuine necessity. So he proceeds more or less according to his planned presentation and nicely gets away with it. But in other instances, the salesman definitely perceives a need to complete his total pitch in just two or three minutes.

When this happens, Walt devotes a larger than usual share of time and energy to his close. He *skips the subtleties,* and comes right out with a forceful and assumptive finish. Immediately after his product pitch, he says, "If that training makes as much sense to you as it does to most of our clients, let's put together a list of your eligible managers and figure out exactly what each one needs. I'll be over next Wednesday at 2 p.m. We'll need an hour." Rather abrupt? *Yes.*

This aggressive close *is* a calculated risk. Walt figures that there probably won't be a second crack at this inaccessible executive—at least not in the foreseeable future. So in effect, he goes for all the marbles. No wishy-washy beating around the bush.

A fast-moving manager can relate to that kind of strongly decisive close and it gets big business for Walt. The shortened presentation comes with a powerfully stated close. But knowing when to *stop* is extremely important.

Avoid Talking Past That "Magic Moment"

Silence is not only magnified by telephone, but it is infinitely more difficult to handle because there are no diversions like eye contact or paper-shuffling to occupy the voids.

The momentary awkwardness that a few seconds of quiet brings is the root cause of a major problem to many telephone salespeople—especially in hurry-up presentations such as the ones just discussed. The caller finally wins an audience with a top manager who has one foot out the office door, on the way to one meeting or another. A condensed presentation is flawlessly delivered . . . a powerhouse close follows . . . *then things begin to fall apart!*

What happens is this: Immediately following the highly assumptive close, the listener may pause. The individual on the other end of the line may be briefly mulling over the caller's proposition or checking the proposed appointment date on a nearby calendar. But instead of rolling with the pause, the seller begins to panic. With that panic comes a compulsion to go on gabbing.

This fear-provoked chatter is, of course, completely spontaneous. As such, it goes on and on, without any meaningful relationship with the issue of an appointment. It is purely unstructured and serves only to distract the prospect who, only a moment earlier, had been on the very edge of agreeing to the caller's offer.

But the "spell" is broken. The highly effective short presentation has evolved into a rambling ten-minute speech, and it is suddenly easy for the prospect to say: "It's been nice talking to you, but I really have to get to that meeting. I'll call you."

When your extra-potent close has been spoken, let the prospect be the next one to talk! Do *not* let a brief silence shatter your composure. Wait for the response! If you do, *it will be affirmative a good percentage of the time.*

Here we have one more very solid point in favor of structured presentations. If your presentation flow diagram indicates empty space after your close, then by all means let there be silence after your close has been delivered. (See Figure 7-2.)

Reva D.'s Referral Chain Gets Her on the Line with Company Presidents

Doing business with large, decentralized companies can be frustrating to a caller. Various divisions, branches, and departments can mean call after call to finally zero in on the correct center-of-influence.

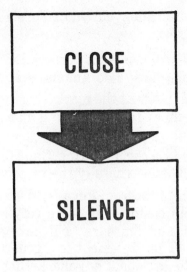

Figure 7-2

At best, the seller progresses through a chain of screens, and eventually ends up talking to the targeted contact. More typically, lower-level managers along the path will intercept the caller and all too often kill the deal. This can happen whether you have identified the ultimate contact or not.

When the seller is stopped short of the objective in this way, it is exceedingly difficult to renew the drive to pay dirt. The caller cannot gracefully go over the head of a manager who said no. That's the quickest possible way to stir up bad feelings in a prospective company.

Reva D. sells a mailing list service to large corporations. In her first year of selling, she was perpetually being shuttled from one department manager to another, and getting turned down somewhere in that seemingly endless chain of screens. Even when she asked for the Vice President of Marketing by name, Reva had to first fight her way up a ladder of people, and usually never did reach her desired contact.

The day Reva began to use her *Referral Chain* strategy, she started reaching decision makers on almost every call.

To illustrate this strategy for you, here's a look at a typical situation:

   A. Reva telephones Ajax Corporation and asks the receptionist for Waldo Adams, V.P. Marketing.

   B. Her call rings at the marketing department and is picked up by the advertising manager's secretary.

   C. Reva introduces herself and again asks for Waldo Adams. "He's in a meeting. Can I take a message for him?" That's generally the response.

   D. The comeback from Reva is, "I *would* leave a message, but customer lists are very important to Mr. Adams, and I'm sure he'll have questions about them." (This statement is a generality that would apply to just about *any* marketing person.)

   E. "Customer Lists?" queries the secretary. "Why can't I connect you to Judy Larson in advertising?" It's not exactly where Reva wants to be, but it *is* a step in the right direction.

   F. Judy is Assistant Advertising Manager. She says, "Jeff (her boss) would like to have information about your service in his file. Send me your literature and I'll make sure he reviews it."
   (To most callers, that's a fatal blow. To Reva, it's just the opening.)

   G. The next day she calls the company again and once more asks for Waldo Adams. But this *time she can drop a few names to try and get her man on the line.* When the advertising secretary answers, the saleswoman says, "I spoke to Jeff's secretary yesterday, and she asked me to get some important information to your company. I'd like to speak with Waldo Adams, please."

This technique *does* distort the facts a bit. But is it any more of a contrived ploy than the practice of putting screens in the path of a caller?

Reva's Referral Chain works like a charm in some cases, but you may prefer to cut through screens with out-and-out boldness.

Using the "Shock Approach" to Blast Through Screens

If you passionately believe in what you are selling, emotion can be summoned and channeled to overcome the obstacles placed before you. The average "screener" just isn't prepared to have a seller come across with a lightning bolt of ultra-strong belief, and sometimes can be swept away by it.

The person standing in your path fully expects a measured and logical attempt to reach the boss. When that is what happens, the typical assistant finds it ridiculously simple to put off even an accomplished caller.

But what happens when the caller dramatically changes pace, and turns on the high voltage? Here's how it might sound:

Screen:	"Good afternoon, Marketing."
You:	"Mrs. Johnson please."
Screen:	"Who's calling?"
You:	"This is Herb Carlson."
Screen:	"What company please?"
You:	"Preston Computer."
Screen:	"May I ask the purpose of your call?"
You:	"We've just introduced a new laser printer I feel would interest Mrs. Johnson."
Screen:	"I don't think she's in the market for a printer, but if you mail some information about it, Mrs. Johnson will review it, and get in touch with you if she has any questions."
You:	(Now to depart drastically from the

> traditional path taken by most tele-
> phone sellers.)
> "I *understand* that you're trying to
> keep most sales calls from Mrs.
> Johnson. But this *is* different, and it's
> important that you understand why.
> We've done studies on how this printer
> performs in conjunction with the com-
> puter system that *your company is us-*
> *ing.* This data might be *extremely* use-
> ful to Mrs. Johnson—and literature
> just won't get the point across.
> "That's why I'd like to have *her* tell me
> *now* if the idea has merit or not."

Strong arguments like this are almost never used to penetrate screens. It will help boost your telephone results when used selectively.

What happens when your contact always seems to be in meetings or on trips when you call?

The Pros and Cons of
Establishing a Call-Back Policy

Many top-earning telephone salespeople are dead set against leaving their names and numbers with a secretary. They feel that return calls are almost never made by prospects. Further, when they *do* occur once in a great while, several things are apt to go wrong. Here are just two ways they can backfire:

- Your contact calls you while you're involved in a telephone presentation with another prospect.
- The call-back comes several days after your initial call, and you can't immediately identify the caller or company. You fumble around and perhaps lose the sale.

The problems all point to one thing: loss of initiative. If *you're* on the receiving end, you are automatically on the defensive . . . and you have to regain control very quickly if you hope to convert the presentation into a sale. But when you initiate the contact, you start with control, and it's far easier to hang onto. In effect, *you* are selecting the time and creating the environment for the interview.

When you do ask a secretary to have his or her boss call you, and it doesn't materialize (as will be the case at least 85 percent of the time), you try again later under somewhat more strained circumstances. Both the secretary *and* boss might feel a little guilty about ignoring you, and they could be a trifle defensive about their failure to do as promised. That won't help your case.

With all its faults, asking for a return call *does* have a place in the scheme of things. When your contact is *absolutely inaccessible,* you might as well try it! And the few times you must try it, make it as spectacular as you can.

Also, leave your name if you intend to call back. This way, when you do follow-up, you won't be a total stranger.

"Baiting the Hook" to Make a Giant Catch

A commercial real estate saleswoman avoids requesting return calls as a rule. But when she does, the note she leaves is almost impossible to disregard. Assuming the people at the prospective company don't know her or the firm she represents, this is the message the woman gives the secretary:

"Please have Mr. Robinson call me at (phone number). It's regarding the expansion of his company."

The secretary invariably tries to pry more information out of the saleswoman, but she gracefully exits without imparting a word more.

If it happens that Robinson's company is on the verge of expansion, there's a 95 percent chance he'll return the call (odds are that *any* established company is expanding at least 10 percent a year). So he calls back, and the real estate woman talks to him about larger office space. She reports that most of the more astute businesspeople admire the innocent ploy.

Try to build a little hook into your request for a return call. If you *have to* ask for a call-back, why not enhance your chances of making it work?

The next tactic for commanding return calls from hard-to-reach prospects is not for everyone, but it definitely does work in this case.

How Gil W. Embarrasses
Ultra-Elusive Prospects Into Responding

On occasion, you may get the distinct feeling that you are being avoided. While most cases of failure to reach the buyer are due to hectic schedules, there *are* people who have enough time to talk, but for their own private reasons treat callers rudely.

Many experienced telephone salespeople prefer to write these ultra-elusive prospects off. But Gil W., an automobile leasing company salesman, figures they do business with *someone,* and it might as well be *him!*

When Gil gets that unmistakable feeling that he's getting a cold shoulder, he'll go out on a limb to obtain a response. He feels that giving up is what most everyone else does, so why not do something provocative to attract a call-back? If it works, he's one of the few who actually *talks* to the ultra-elusive prospect, and if it doesn't work, nothing is lost.

The most provocative tactic the salesman has devised that stops short of offending anyone is as follows:

Please tell Mr. Hurley that just because he's over-paying on car leases now is no reason to discriminate against other leasing company salesmen!"

If Hurley *is* leasing now—and if the above message reaches him intact—it can hit him hard enough to evoke a call-back. Gil claims a success rate of nearly 40 percent. Considering the stubborn refusal of some people when it comes to returning calls, that's respectable. The salesman adds that most of the returned calls are from amused executives who admire his rather audacious approach! Still, use this tactic *only* if there are no other alternatives open to you.

Hard-to-reach prospects will always be with us, as will tough-to-sell prospects. The coming chapter provides valuable advice on how to use fundamental telephone sales strategies to beef up your general effectiveness, no matter how difficult your market is.

fail-safe telephone sales approaches that close tough customers

It's naive to think that the same basic telephone presentation will work with equal effectiveness on *all* prospects in a variety of markets. An accountant, after all, will probably require a different philosophical slant than, say, the operator of an auto parts business.

The product or service in question will also lend itself more or less favorably to a given approach. The discipline of telephone selling is not that "cut and dried" where you can consult a chart to determine the optimum type of sell for a specific combination of circumstances.

Custom-Tailor Your Total Delivery to Get Even the Most Difficult Orders

It takes testing to identify the best way to go: should you use a *positive* sell? A consultant's approach? Will your prospects sell *themselves* with just a bit of gentle prodding from you . . . or do they need slam-bang closes prefaced by highly assumptive presentations?

Whatever the answer finally turns out to be, it's easy to adjust your structured presentation to embody the most effective approach. Each basic type is described in the following pages.

Even if you have already identified the best possible way to handle the prospects in your market, the following approaches will broaden your arsenal of sales tactics. You never know when that unusually tough prospect will come along—the one who doesn't match the typical pattern.

Minnie D.'s Negative Sell Nets Her $210 a Day

Minnie sells secretarial courses by telephone. She sets appointments for the school's field sales representatives. Needless to say, the people who close sales don't want to waste their time on weak appointments.

Minnie's first four months in the business were marked by canceled appointments, "no-shows," shoppers who had no intention to enter training, and every other imaginable kind of bad appointment. Her telephone skills were being seriously questioned by both the salespeople and school management.

The woman's approach had been generally positive. She felt that anyone contemplating continued education needed encouragement and support. So Minnie had used a soft sell, sprinkled liberally with optimism. She stressed the future, and how it would be bright for those who prepared for it.

It suddenly dawned on Minnie that she had been incredibly naive. The average vocational school prospect did not respond strongly to encouragement, but did react to a *challenge*.

This new *negative approach* took all the self-discipline the saleswoman could muster. But she was determined to make the drastic 180-degree change from her soft, sweet telephone presentation *to one that forced a prospect into action.* Her new negatively-slanted presentation includes the following strong challenges to each prospect:

- "Did you continue your education after high school graduation?" If not, "why?"
- "What were your grades as a senior?"
- "Do you think you could maintain a tough school and study schedule now?"
- "Are you considering any other fields?" If so, "What do you see as the pros and cons of each?"
- "Are you sure you're not just looking at the glamour aspects of being a secretary?"

The prospect had to fight through a string of unveiled challenges. The strong prospects "survived," and were told by Minnie that the final hurdle remaining was a visit from a field representative who would *personally* evaluate the person's chances.

There are no more complaints about the quality of Minnie's appointments. She's the school's leading caller, and she averages commissions of $210 a day!

Robie W.'s Positive Sell
Boosts Her Sales 375 Percent in One Year

The opposite side of the coin is a sell characterized by encouragement. It's the approach Minnie used before she discovered the power of *challenging* potential students. It works for her.

Robie can't use anything that even *resembles* negativity in her telephone presentation for a quality catering service. For as long a time as she can recall, prospects for this service have responded to the *positive approach* of reassurance, meticulous explanations about food preparation and, above all, extreme patience from the caller.

The saleswoman has, at different times, tested approaches that were decidedly negative in nature. In one instance, she cast subtle aspersions at a competitive caterer by describing what a catastrophe could result from badly handled food preparation. Robie was later convinced that this tactic succeeded only in frightening a few people out of using *any* caterer!

As clearly as a purely positive sell was indicated for her business, negative elements continued to creep into Robie's telephone approach. In one case, it repeatedly came up at the close:

Prospect: "That seems to be pretty much what we need for the party. I'll call you in a few days with our order."

Robie: "We might not be able to handle it in a few days. It takes about a week for us to get ready for a party like yours."

Robie's rather simple statement of fact was *loaded* with negative implications:

- She didn't intend it, but the *impression* of her words was, "If you don't order *today,* don't bother."
- To some prospects, the statement may have conveyed that sandwiches sat around in the catering company's kitchens for a few days. Robie failed to mention that the one week of lead time was needed to acquire *the ingredients*.
- The sudden transition from a supportive, encouraging attitude to a challenging, almost sulking remark, didn't help Robie's credibility. It was as if her earlier patience had been nothing but a strategy calculated to make a sale.

Let's look at a response stated in totally *positive* terms, more characteristic of Robie's methods:

Prospect: "That seems to be pretty much what we need for the party. I'll call you in a few days with our order."

> Robie: "Great! We'd love to work with you!
> But don't forget to let us know at least
> a week before the party so we can order
> the choicest cuts and assure that
> everything is perfect."

That conclusion is thoroughly positive. It leaves Robie's prospect with strong feelings of confidence, yet a sense of urgency.

Although Minnie and Robie have arrived at telephone approaches as opposite as they can be, and both are enjoying optimum results by remaining completely faithful to the selling style that works in their market, it is possible to combine negative and positive techniques if it appears advantageous to do so.

Using the "Attitude Approach" in Preparing Prospects for Easy Closes

"Reading" the spirit of your prospect is the first big step toward using positive or negative telephone tactics effectively. If you can accurately gauge the *attitude* of the other person, you can quickly select an approach that will work.

A loan officer with quotas to meet uses telephone power-selling principles to control discussions with people who call to inquire about borrowing cash. When a prospect sounds anxious or apprehensive, the banker becomes decidedly positive and reassuring. But when the inquirer is remote and aloof, the officer goes into a negative mode to present a challenge.

As a general rule, the *closer* a prospect is to buying, the more negative you can afford to be.

> Prospect: "It sure *seems* that your remodeling
> plans are everything I want."
>
> You: "Look, nobody is ever absolutely posi-
> tive. The outcome will depend a lot on
> how much time and energy *you're*
> willing to commit to the project."

Most salespeople tend to become exceedingly weak at the close. Weakness usually comes across as extreme agreeability; *everything* the prospect says is okay. The seller stops expressing opinions out of fear that the deal will cave in.

The fact is, the close is the time to get a little tougher. You become a little tougher by giving your words a bit of negative flavor. Remember, *challenge* brings out emotion in most people. It pushes them into action they might not take under ordinary circumstances.

Again, to be in a position to successfully mix positive and negative, *you have to "feel" the mood of the prospect!* The *attitude approach* demands professional-level listening from the caller.

John E.'s Key to Making Unsolicited Calls Pay Off Big

John operates a small business that supplies typewriter and adding machine ribbons to companies in an East Coast city. All of his sales are generated through telephone contact. Some 60 percent of the orders are obtained by *outgoing* calls to lists of local firms. The rest are calls to his office prompted by advertising. John describes the latter group—the incoming calls—as unsolicited because he does not initiate the contact.

Although calls of the unsolicited variety are usually most of the way to a sale, John handles them with emphatic negativity. He asks questions like . . .

- "Are you *sure* you want premium quality?"
- "Do you understand that our terms are cash-on-delivery because of our discount structure?"
- "You *do* understand that our minimum order is $100, don't you?"

And so forth. In John's estimation, an incoming order like this has been pre-sold to a great extent. Therefore, he is convinced that he actually *strengthens* the relationship through a little polite negativity. John says:

"By the time I'm finished with an unsolicited caller, the person knows that we're the most thorough ribbon supplier in this area. They know that our concern goes deeper than just taking an order!"

Would a *positive* approach work as well on unsolicited calls? It might, but John is personally sold on the fact that the supportive technique is best for outgoing cold calls, and the technique of challenging is ideal for buyers who come to *him*.

For you it might be different. The answer is to *test* before you decide.

Turning Complaints and Service Calls Into Major Profits

While we're on the subject of tough customers, it's timely to discuss a variety of incoming calls that most businesspeople dread—the complaint and service call.

Many of the most successful companies and individual business operators regard routine gripes and requests for help as one big nuisance. They deal with the problem efficiently enough, but completely fail to look beyond the immediate situation in order to perceive the opportunities. For example, when a customer—even an irate one—calls in with a problem, and it is resolved by a company representative to a point of absolute satisfaction, *the relationship between company and customer is at an extremely high level.* Bidding farewell without making an attempt to make a sale is a waste of opportunity; it's a level of goodwill that may not be easy to duplicate in the future.

For very small firms, such as those where the owner might do the selling, accounting, and handling of problem calls, there is more of a likelihood that happy endings will turn into new orders. But a larger organization may have a separate service group, and that is very probably an area of missed chances.

As a way of protecting against a passive service department like the one just described, heavy training in telephone selling is a top priority. The people taking complaints and service calls could be nonselling technicians who don't know the first thing about a close. But they should be trained in at least the fundamental steps of the telephone presentation structure described earlier.

As soon as the service folks gain a little confidence in the simple steps that make a phone sale, they'll start turning satisfied customers into enthusiastic buyers!

Dormant customers are closely related to problem callers, and deserve a look at this point.

Winning Back Inactive Customers

When you have a spare moment, check back into your old records and make a list of past good customers who are not buying from you today. There is little doubt that if you could recapture, say, 20 percent of them, your income would soar.

Despite the above fact, it *is* true that many business operators make only a token attempt to correct a bad situation that is unfolding, and threatens to wreck a business relationship. When events have finally reached an impossible stage, the seller usually turns away from the mess in favor of cultivating fresh, new clients.

Too often, a demolished seller/buyer association is loaded with injured pride and bruised ego. Neither side will yield, and the result is anger and frustration, then eventually a wrenching break.

What lots of marketers don't realize is this: Most customers are gravely inconvenienced when a supplier falls out. Price agreements become invalid, stock flow is disrupted, and the buyer has to spend time and effort lining up a new source that often doesn't pan out as well.

It *pays* to make a valiant effort to save a deteriorating

relationship. The telephone simplifies the task immensely. A very good way to do it is to build a step-by-step structure. Do it the same basic way you design one for the purpose of making sales, but instead of qualification questions, you probe for reasons why things are going poorly. Such questions might relate to:

- Delivery — Has it been satisfactory?
- Quality — Whether a product or service, has it been up to standard?
- Price — Are we still competitive?
- Service — Are problems getting resolved?

A structured telephone approach will save a customer who is losing interest or one who is already dormant. It helps you *identify the root cause of the problem,* and it provides the specific tactics you can use to return things to normal. The structure also *prevents a discussion from becoming emotional,* which is a major stumbling block when handling problems.

The "Consultation Approach" Is a Proven Money-Maker for Telephone Pro Mickey T.

Just about every seasoned telephone sales veteran experiences an occasional "super skeptic." The finely honed sensitivity of the accomplished caller picks up one of the following unspoken signals early in the conversation:

- "I don't trust anyone who takes an obvious *seller's* point of view in a presentation."
- "I don't trust anyone who takes *my* point of view in an effort to make a sale."

No matter which approach you take, you are likely to lose when you deal with this extremely tough prospect. Mickey T., a franchise salesman, encountered this phenomenon frequently and was nearly defeated by it.

His is a major sale, requiring a $25,000 down payment and a commitment for $20,000 more. When that much cash is involved, the prospect tends to get a bit sensitive about a salesperson's motives. (Is this peddler just looking for a fat commission, without any regard at all for my welfare? Or, is he taking my side just to be patronizing?)

At first, Mickey tried switching from one approach to the other in his telephone sales effort. But the overly suspicious "super skeptics" reacted negatively to both methods.

Finally, he tried taking a totally neutral position. Mickey called it his *consultation approach*. It meticulously avoided *any* partiality in favor of either his deal or of the prospect's feelings. In other words, the salesman acted as a disinterested advisor, almost like a top-level stockbroker discussing the pros and cons of various securities with a concerned client.

In his telephone calls to prospective franchisees, Mickey pursued a course designed to legitimately match a specific individual to a well-defined business opportunity. It was a smooth blending of positive and negative, *never* reflecting favoritism to the shopper or to his employer.

In a traditional sense, there is very little selling in this manner of presenting a package. But in a purely practical sense, the prospect quickly gets the feeling that Mickey is telling it the way it really is—without embellishment of any kind.

When a big commission check is at stake, the salesman admits to fighting off an occasional temptation to depart from his impartial position and take a more typical "company man" role. But he remains in the consultation approach because he knows *it offers the best possible chance to close the super skeptics.*

How to Make Prospects Sell Themselves

The consultation approach by telephone makes a tough prospect feel as if there is no influence being exerted. This especially skeptical individual is impressed with the fact that the caller is merely supplying raw data on which a judgment can be based.

That brings up one more very effective telephone sales approach, also calculated to help your contact come to a favorable conclusion without prodding. The approach is simply to *give your prospect credit for having a little intelligence!*

How many times have *you* been on the receiving end of a sales presentation (by telephone or in-person), and felt "talked down to"? Every conclusion was made for you, and nothing whatsoever was left to your imagination. In fact, if solid, basic facts alone had been supplied, you could have used your imagination to arrive at stronger conclusions than the seller did!

That, in part, is what Mickey T. does in his consultation approach; he stops short of drawing the whole picture for his prospect, and he lets the person's imagination do the final job of selling.

An insensitive caller refuses to acknowledge that anyone else has the insight to see as far as the horizon. This type of seller overdescribes just about every point, and succeeds in squelching the prospect's perception of product or service benefits.

Try telling less. Forget all the obsolete warnings you've heard about spoon-feeding even the most sophisticated buyers. Build your telephone presentation to *stimulate* your listener's creativity. For example, instead of saying:

> "Our Ajax copier's speed will reduce the wait, and save money because your people won't be standing around as long."

Say:

> "Knowing the internal copy bottlenecks as well as you do, I'm sure you have a dozen ideas on how the Ajax will cut costs."

Tougher buyers usually will respond well to a mature approach like this. These people *want* to see the light on their own, and resist someone who tries to lead them by the hand!

Difficult buyers will also respond to solid merchandising. A special offer built into your telephone presentation can make an enormous difference in your business. Let's look at a few of the ways it can be done.

merchandising strategies that guarantee big-profit orders by phone

9

A close look at the world's major retailers reveals ingenious merchandising. Every department in a successful store is up to something that will stir shoppers into a buying frame of mind. Even the traffic pattern is laid out to maximize impulse purchases.

The fastest growing industrial companies also merchandise adeptly. Some of them have learned from clever retailers and increase their profits by offering specials.

Pack Your Offer with Special Drama and Appeal

Any business can immediately benefit by putting more excitement into its sales effort, but only a very small number incorporate special buying inducements into telephone operations. For some mysterious reason, they don't hesitate to put zip into their direct mail and magazine ads, but suddenly become sedate when prospects are reached by telephone!

This chapter describes how an assortment of astute merchandisers add tremendous wallop to their telephone presentations. It also provides ideas on merchandising programs you can probably adapt to your power-selling strategy with surprising ease.

The real essence of using good merchandising intelligently in your telephone work is this:

> *Getting an opportunity to address your market directly is of monumental value. The telephone presents that golden opportunity more effectively than any other known method of communication. As long as you have that amazingly potent tool working for you, why not give each direct contact all the drama and appeal you possibly can?*

How Special Accessory Packages Set Telephone Sales Records for a Tool Distributor

Marketing management of this midwest company was ordered by its Board of Directors to achieve a 25 percent increase in gross sales for the second half, which was to begin in just 30 days. Obviously, such a boost would depend on the rapid implementation of a very strong sales-generating program.

In weighing the available options during a series of meetings, the sales and marketing staff was unanimous in seeing the telephone and direct mail as the primary means of attaining the improved totals. But the question of *how* these attacks would be utilized was not easily answered; both approaches had been used by the firm on a steady basis, and a sharp increase in results over the six-month period was just not perceived.

An answer didn't present itself until the marketing people took a close look at the mechanics of their existing telephone sales operation. Four people were permanently assigned to handle incoming phone orders. This group was so busy processing requests for tools, there was no time available for them to even think about add-on sales from new buyers. Add-on sales was an area that had been totally neglected by the distributor, and one that held the potential to bring about the demanded increase. The following example typified the problem.

A buyer of heavy-duty soldering equipment would *certainly* be a prime candidate for solder, safety goggles, and a long list of other accessories essential to the basic process. Yet up until now, an order for the main item was cheerfully taken, and the customer bid farewell by the order-taker!

Management could only assume that hundreds, and possibly thousands of buyers, were buying high-profit accessories from various local sources as the need arose. It was finally recognized that a little fundamental merchandising had to be applied to capture that business.

The Manager of Marketing Services was given the task of coming up with a specific program. Here's the mechanics of the approach he used.

Bruce L.'s Priceless Tips on Packaging Products for Telephone Sales

In just 48 hours, Bruce came up with a series of packages that would break every sales record at the tool company in less than 90 days. The program *assured* that the ambitious sales projections set by the Board of Directors would be *exceeded*.

The marketing man's concept was ingenious because it avoided price reductions that would negatively impact profits. Instead, it utilized *existing* resources and systems.

Bruce sifted through the tool company's entire product array and organized it into *packages* instead of individual items. Families of products were listed wherever possible and would be offered to buyers in just that way.

For example, an electric drill would *not* simply be considered a stand-alone product. It would be presented as an integrated package, accompanied by various bits, sanding attachments, and so forth. The customer could, of course, buy the basic drill alone, but not before the whole family of items was offered at a group price (which was merely the aggregate of all individual items, and *not* a discounted sum).

All telephone order people were equipped with a notebook. In each, the various packages were alphabetized for quick reference. A person calling in an order would *instantly* be offered not just the primary product, but the planned package which included all the related accessories and options.

Through the initial 60 days of operation, it turned out that fully 32 percent of new telephone buyers bought the entire package. Some 15 percent more purchased selected extras, and the rest placed orders for the basic item only.

The boost in revenue *easily* gave this tool firm its targeted 25 percent increase. But equally important, *the new program turned thousands of customers into regular buyers of supplies they had been buying from other sources!*

Interestingly, the company's telephone order people agree that the *package price* they quote is almost always considered a special by customers, even though it's the normal total of all package items. Somehow, a "package deal" looks like a bargain, whether it is or not. *That's* good merchandising!

How You Can Use Human Nature to Make a Personal Fortune By Telephone

As we've just seen, many shoppers hear the term "package deal" and immediately read the word "bargain" into the offer. The fact is, successful merchandising is aimed at certain characteristics possessed by all human beings.

For example:

Laziness makes the concept of a package deal attractive to most buyers. The necessity of thinking about and searching for other required components is removed. That work has been done by someone else.

"Package deal" sounds like "bargain" because the concept of many components being offered at one price has traditionally signified value. The favorable connotation is always present, whether the value is there or not!

Greed makes shoppers respond to premium offers. A well-known company that sells products to advertising managers by telephone uses the greed factor to maximum advantage. They give away a gift to these managers every time they receive an order. Since their product is virtually identical to those produced by competitive firms, that gift is undoubtedly the reason for their supremacy. More about this telephone merchandising strategy a bit later.

Exclusivity sells tons of goods via telephone. Call it "snob appeal" if you prefer. By any title, it's a super way to capture a status-conscious or ego-oriented market. A leather goods entrepreneur makes a fortune by building up the self-importance of executives. His fascinating telephone methods are described for you in this chapter.

Insecurity opens up vast opportunities for telephone merchandising. Most people are basically fearful of loss. If an offer can somehow provoke those emotions, and then provide protection against loss, it is likely to be effective.

One example is a seller of property insurance, who accomplishes a major part of his sale by phone. He jolts his prospect into a state of heightened attentiveness by describing the exact amount of real estate appreciation that has occurred in the person's neighborhood. He then relates a case where a fire in the area recently destroyed a home, and the owners were insured at appraisal levels of the past. The loss was shocking—and impressed his prospects as few other examples could.

Good merchandising is simply the ability to *verbally package* a telephone presentation in an attractive way. That packaging has to be aimed at the very heart of some basic human motivation like greed, fear of loss, or some other inherent "hot button."

The case histories that follow illustrate how effective merchandising is accomplished by a group of successful telephone pros.

How Kathleen N.'s "Hot Button" Merchandising Technique Wins Big Ticket Telephone Sales

Kathleen sells word-processing machines by telephone. It's a high-priced product in an extremely competitive market, so she has to know how to locate quickly a prospect's "hot button," then package her presentation to reach that emotion.

The saleswoman discovered early that *every* prospective company had some exceptionally important applications for word-processing. Her competitors were aware of applications, but rarely merchandised their equipment with a strong thrust toward those specific uses. They approached each prospective firm in a very general way.

In contrast, Kathleen knew that a company controller was apt to get emotional about the flood of collection letters that had to be manually prepared each month. She had figures ready to dramatize the time-saving if the chore could be automated. And she knew that a Marketing Manager faced horrendous correspondence problems that her system could take care of. The savings were illustrated in graph form for extra drama.

The saleswoman had not only quantified the advantages of word-processing on an industry-by-industry and task-by-task basis, but she also made it a point to learn more about the nature of specific projects with which her potential customers were involved.

When Kathleen made a call to a particular company, *she was in a position to ask for a person in a specialized job. She could then converse with that individual in terms of very definite problems and solutions.*

While her rivals were delivering meaningless generalities, Kathleen was getting to the core of the matter and was thus touching emotions. Her "hot button" merchandising made her an industry sales leader.

A chemical salesman uses gifts to sell more effectively by telephone.

Premiums Put Ray V. on the Way to Wealth

Ray sells chemicals used by manufacturers in a variety of applications. He uses the telephone extensively to obtain orders in a 15-state area. There are four major chemical companies, and a host of smaller firms, marketing to the same group of potential buyers. In view of that extremely stiff competitive picture, Ray believes that establishing both his personal identity, and the identity of his product, are vital.

Product quality is a relatively minor point since all formulations on the market are generally comparable. Each plant buyer should get to know *who* Ray is and should remember the various chemical designations in his line if he is to successfully obtain and keep a foothold in the market.

In this instance, *merely calling a prospect repeatedly was not sufficient*. The information he imparted during telephone presentations quickly got lost among the thousands of other products buyers worked with. Ray decided he needed a far more dramatic way to establish identification. Ray decided to try gifts to reinforce his message.

For every call he made to a qualified prospect, successful or not, Ray sent the buyer a pocket appointment guide, a fancy pen, or other premium in the wholesale price range of $2 or less. Each was imprinted with his name and company name, plus as much product information as space allowed. Each small gift was accompanied by a letter that described a better item the buyer could get when a purchase was made. Ray then filed each of these prospect's letters for later follow-up.

For each order he received, the buyer received from Ray a product that ran in the $10 wholesale range. These included various carefully selected small appliances, desktop accessories, and other gifts he was certain would be useful and appreciated.

As desired, the salesman's undistinguished chemical offer suddenly gained distinction! *Nearly every buyer began associating Ray's name and products to personal gain.* They bought from him simply because a gift was *always* part of the deal!

Is the cost of his gift program a limiting factor? Ray insists it is not. He provides these figures:

Telephone calls in
one typical day 15   ($30 in $2 gifts)

Closes in
one typical day . . . . .1.5   ($15 in $10 gifts)

The average profit in a chemical sale is $240. Thus, 1.5 per day gives Ray about $360 . . . easily enough to cover the cost of gifts, especially considering that it's his primary means of promotion. And that doesn't take into account the *growth* of his business since he started the program.

How Paul C. Creates
Power-Merchandising for Telephone

Normally, the leather goods business tends to be a passive one. Retail operators advertise, then primarily wait for store traffic to develop into sales. Paul C. always viewed that as a backward approach, so he developed an astutely merchandised attack, using the telephone as his main thrust.

First, he zeroed in on medium sized to large sized businesses as a test market for his idea. Paul perceived in that group a rich source of executives, secretaries, and other employees who would want attaché cases and other leather goods custom-imprinted with their company's logo.

From a merchandising standpoint, the concept was sound for the following reasons:

- Most firms would welcome the idea of having their employees carry briefcases, wallets, and checkbook covers emblazoned with company identification. It was simply good public relations. That being the case, any progressive organization could be expected to help promote the idea.

- Penetration of area companies would inevitably lead to increased traffic in the leather store. Expanded customer awareness *always* meant more sales in Paul's opinion.

His merchandising strategy was actually based on people's desire to be *different* . . . to have some kind of exclusivity. A stamped, embossed, or engraved design on an attractive leather case was decidedly different from those almost everyone else carried.

On the strength of that belief in how people would react, Paul launched his program. He personally made no less than 15 calls a day to company presidents and other top executives. By the two-week mark, he had shown sample-imprinted leather goods to six highly qualified prospects. By month's end, he bagged $4,200 in added sales generated by the calling. Store sales were up nearly 30 percent over the prior year's totals.

One man's realization that egos would be inflated by reproducing company logos on functional leather items successfully translated into a money-making program. It is an example of masterful merchandising, implemented quickly and economically by telephone.

The "Free Demo" System That Rocketed Ella K. to New Earning Records

Ella K. is today the top sales producer for a company that makes a computer disk-cleaning machine. For years,

the firm had been encountering difficulty in closing telephone sales. A typical prospect was reluctant to make a
commitment for a high-priced unit that he or she had never
seen in action. The manufacturer was resisting the expense
of establishing a field sales force, so sales had to be made via
telephone.

The young woman, who was at that time a sales department clerk, observed that the *benefits* of the cleaning
machine were difficult to get across. You could *describe* the
fact that perfectly clean data storage disks improved performance, but unless that benefit was actually *demon-
strated,* the point was never quite driven home.

After giving the problem some thought, Ella came up
with the merchandising strategy that was to completely
turn her employer's company around. She suggested a simple "free demo" arrangement whereby the prospect could
obtain a machine for 15-days without obligation to purchase.
They would then clean all the disks that had been given up
as too old and dirty for continued use.

Management saw the potential and agreed to test the
program. Three reconditioned units were designated as
demos, and in several days each of them was mailed to
prospective companies by prior arrangement. By month's
end, two of the firms requested new cleaners to replace the
demos, and the third returned their demo unit.

The cost of mailing totaled less than $30, while the
profit on the two sales was $1,400. Both buying companies
were astonished at how quickly the cleaner restored their
used disks to like-new condition! Ella's plan provided live
proof of a capability people never quite believed existed;
experiencing it *themselves* made the difference.

The manufacturer now has up to 20 demo cleaners out
at any given time. Two-thirds of them consistently convert to
sales, an improvement of 76 percent compared to the pre-
demo days.

Telephone power-selling, plus Ella's ingenious merchandising approach, made this borderline company a suc-

cess, and turned a sales department clerk into a marketing leader.

Vital Keys to Make Your Offer Almost Irresistible

Ella's idea of sending out a demonstration machine so a prospective buyer can spend some time actually *using* the product and *experiencing* its benefits is widely and successfully utilized today in the world of telephone marketing.

In just about every case where a free demo is used, the telephone caller has to be every bit as thorough in creating a telephone presentation to fully qualify *serious* buyers. In this way, the demo does not preclude the necessity of building prospect interest. One more thing: The concept of a guarantee takes on magnified importance when you use any kind of free demo approach. The following points should *never* be overlooked:

- The seller must somehow provide comfort that *continued support* will be rendered. One of a prospect's deepest fears is that a telephone transaction will be "hit and run." Lots of credibility has to be established!
- A *formal* assurance of performance and quality should be provided to potential buyers. Perhaps a printed guarantee or warranty can be sent as soon as a phone call is ended.

The need to provide assurance of this kind is definitely not limited to small, unknown companies. Large corporations marketing popular products or service must also show that they'll be around to stand behind their sale.

Remember, a buyer who consummates a purchase from an established store or other distribution outlet feels that the people who are physically present in that place will take the responsibility for problems that may develop later. This belief may be totally unfounded, *but it does exist.*

But a telephone caller, whether he or she represents a Fortune 500 company or a one-person business, is merely a disembodied voice. As far as the prospect is concerned, the seller may be out there in a phone booth somewhere with the products stuffed into the trunk of a car!

A guarantee is decidedly a facet of good merchandising, especially when you close the sale by phone or offer a free demo as Ella does.

How to Select the Right Merchandising Strategy for Your Business

There are infinite numbers of products and services that lend themselves to telephone sales. Along with that, the possible merchandising methods that can be applied are also nearly endless. Facing this bewildering array of choices, how do you formulate the proper attack?

The following steps will almost always get you to the optimum answer:

● *Ask yourself how YOU would prefer to buy.* If you didn't possess solid instincts about the world of commerce, you wouldn't be in a business environment today. The fact is, you *are* a perceptive judge of tactics, and you *can* discern the strong from the ineffective. That being the case, sit back and think of ways your product or service could be made more appealing.

If you received a phone call right now from someone selling your deal, try to imagine how it could be offered to be truly buyable. What would it take to get *you* excited about it?

● *Keep an eye on competitors.* Being absolutely original when you formulate a merchandising strategy *is not necessary*. Why constantly reinvent the wheel? Most of the time-proven tactics have been used in varying forms for as long as anybody can remember.

Therefore, your competitors—or people in related businesses—are probably using some very successful merchandising programs. You can easily adapt the best ones for *your* telephone presentation. After all, that's exactly what *they* did!

Make a list of companies similar to yours and find out how they sell. Then analyze the tactics you like most to see if they'll fit your operation.

● *Test a select group of approaches.* You'll emerge from the first two steps with a few favored merchandising approaches in mind. The first step is to *test* each of them for effectiveness.

The management section of this book provides valuable guidelines on conducting tests.

While you are searching for good merchandising tactics, don't forget the *obvious* things that get sales by telephone. The following case study illustrates that point.

Exposing Other Products and Services Nets Tom G. $75,000 a Year

For some six years, Tom bumped along in his remodeling business, earning between $30,000 and $35,000 yearly. Approximately 70 percent of his business was generated by incoming calls originating from classified telephone directory inquiries and referrals.

People would call, ask for quotes on interior painting, and either engage Tom's services or fall to competitors. Quite normal up to that point.

The problem was this: As Tom continued in business year after year, the scope of his services gradually expanded to include custom draperies, paperhanging, carpeting, and wall paneling. But Tom had become so accustomed to talking about painting, he usually failed to even *mention* the other services. And the workers who went out to complete projects for him never got that involved. The only time Tom ever sold a nonpainting service was when a telephone inquirer specifically *asked* if he offered it!

Then, in his sixth year of operation, Tom suddenly started doing the obvious. *Every* incoming lead was taken through the total "shopping list" of interior services his company performed. No matter *what* callers were interested in, they got a total rundown of Tom's capabilities.

Obvious? Absolutely! But you'd be astonished at how many firms get so engrossed with *one* item that they sacrifice other important revenue producers.

In Tom's case, the extra minute or two he now spends on each call pays a total of almost $100,000 in gross sales annually. That translates to a *doubling* of Tom's personal income!

To capitalize on his new-found merchandising tactic, Tom started going back and calling prior customers to expose them to his other services. To do that, Tom devised a simple but effective follow-up system. Let's look at that important area right now, beginning with vital program controls.

phone-selling controls to build an automatic business-producing machine

includes sample forms!

If your telephone selling effort is directed to consumers, the wisdom of keeping a call record for every contact you make is debatable. The required filling in of names, addresses, and other data might turn out to be a task that cuts into your calling time—especially when you encounter "not interested" parties whom you'll probably never contact again.

How to Take Charge of Your Power-Selling Program

A direct-to-consumer caller definitely should keep records on those prospects who, for one reason or another, will be ready to buy later. The all-too-often practice is to schedule follow-up calls by means of notes on napkins and other miscellaneous scraps of paper that invariably get lost or are ignored when a call-back is due from you.

If you call business establishments in your telephone sales effort, *the keeping of a record for every company qualified to buy from you is an absolute necessity!*

In business-to-business selling, even flat-out rejections can suddenly turn into receptive buyers a month or a year later. All it takes is a change of company philosophy, a personnel switch, or a new product from you that is eagerly accepted. A "cold" prospect is never really "dead."

The truth is, the really substantial sales volume written by accomplished telephone sellers is done on *follow-up calls.* Most pros, whether they deal with consumers or businesses, will tell you that the practice of tracking good, but "not-quite-ready" prospects, pays major profits.

There is simply *no* satisfactory way to accurately track these budding buyers except by keeping a comprehensive record on each one. The following pages describe forms for telephone selling controls that have been exhaustively tested and proven by both small operators and major corporations.

The Prospect Form: A Vital Tool
for Profitable Telephone Sales

Figure 10-1 is a form you can use for just about any type of prospect. It can easily be modified to fit your specific needs. The following suggestions will help you use the form to optimum effectiveness:

A. **Source of Inquiry.** *Every* lead should be attributed to a definite source. That's the only way you'll ever get a picture of which promotional efforts and media are doing the most good. Sourcing lets you accentuate the effective advertising and eliminate any programs that are not pulling their weight.

Outgoing "cold calls" don't have a source in the same

TELEPHONE CONTACT FORM

Date: _____   Contact by Priority:

Source of Inquiry: _____   1. _____

                                         2. _____

Company: _____   3. _____

Address: _____   4. _____

City _____ State _____ Zip _____

Telephone (____) _____

QUALIFICATION

COMMENTS _____
_____
_____
_____
_____
_____
_____
_____
_____

☐ PROSPECT RATING

FOLLOW-UP ACTION RECORD

DATE	TALKED TO	COMMENTS	SEND	APP'T	CALL AGAIN	OTHER

Figure 10-1

sense that incoming inquiries do, but you *can* track the lists you are using. For example, is a Chamber of Commerce business directory yielding more qualified appointments than calls you make from a local telephone book?

B. **Complete Address Information.** If you deal with consumers, simply eliminate the *company* line. In any event, be sure you get *all* mailing data. Verify it with your prospect, since it is easy to transpose numbers, which causes delays.

C. **Contact By Priority.** Get the consumer's *full* name and verify it for correct spelling.

If you deal with other companies, do the same as above, but list *everyone* in the buying loop in order of their importance in decision making; top person is number one, and so on down the line. Don't forget to include secretaries and administrative assistants, too. It's extremely helpful to address them by name when you make follow-up calls.

One more tip: If a name is difficult to pronounce correctly, *write out the phonetic sound* so you don't stumble on it every time you call. For example, the name Margette M. Hronech is entered as it should be, but next to it you would print: Mar-Jet M. Rah-nek. First, be absolutely positive how the person *likes* to have it pronounced.

D. **Qualifications.** Whatever qualifications you finally devise for your telephone presentation should be reproduced in this part of the Contact Form. This will give you a permanent profile of the prospect.

Figure 10-2 shows how a precision machine manufacturing company set up its qualification section.

E. **Prospect Rating.** After you go through the qualification questions, you can ascertain a prospect's readiness-to-buy. This is translated to a prioritized rating, "A" through "D", as described earlier in this book. This rating will dictate how the prospect is to be handled in terms of follow-up. The next chapter goes into detail on call-backs.

F. **Comments.** In this section, you *supplement* the answers you receive from qualification questions in order to

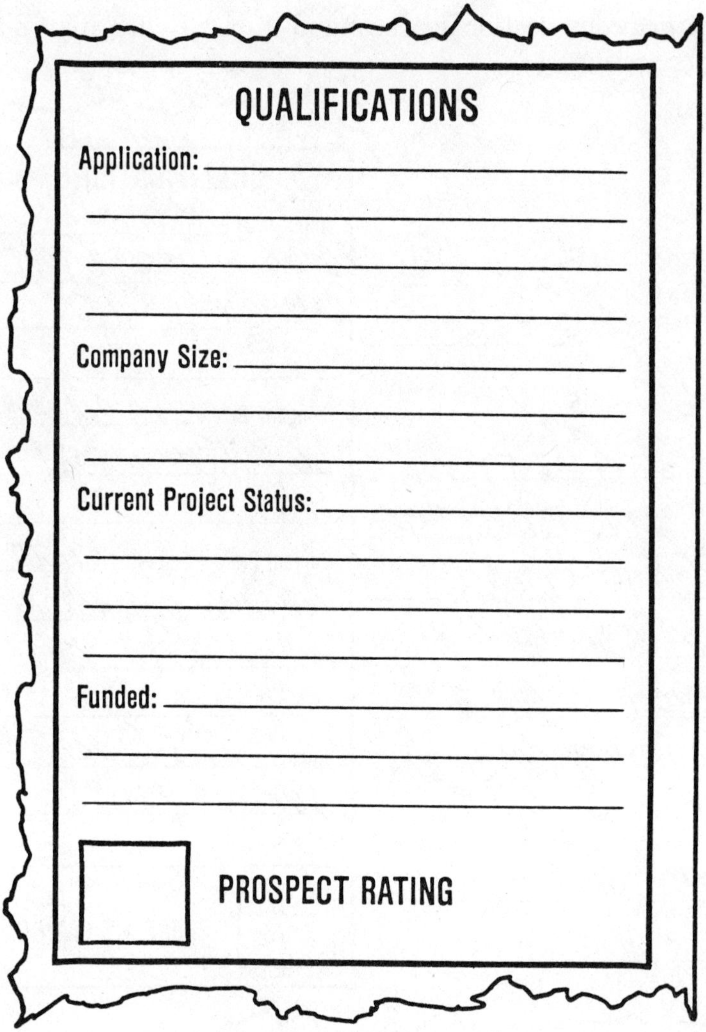
QUALIFICATIONS

Application: ______________________

Company Size: ______________________

Current Project Status: ______________________

Funded: ______________________

PROSPECT RATING

Figure 10-2

get a total picture of your prospect's needs. There are always statements from your prospect that should be noted for future reference.

To see the way this might work, Figure 10-3 provides an illustration of how the precision machine manufacturer's

Qualifications section works hand-in-hand with his *Comments* section.

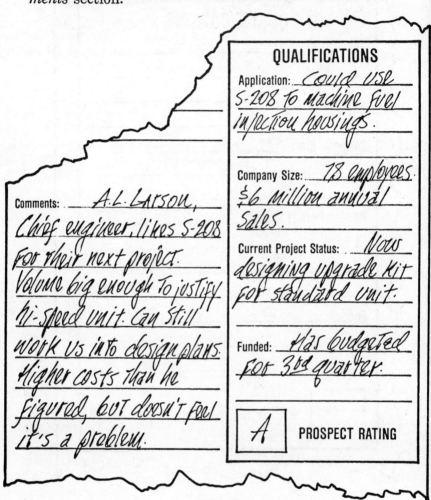

QUALIFICATIONS

Application: *Could use S-208 to machine fuel injection housings.*

Company Size: *78 employees. $6 million annual sales.*

Current Project Status: *Now designing upgrade kit for standard unit.*

Funded: *Has budgeted for 3rd quarter.*

Comments: *A.L. Larson, Chief engineer, likes S-208 for their next project. Volume big enough to justify hi-speed unit. Can still work us into design plans. Higher costs than he figured, but doesn't feel it's a problem.*

A   **PROSPECT RATING**

Figure 10-3

Using Your "Comments" Section to Maximum Effect

With very little writing, you can capture the essence of a prospect's situation. It does not take a lengthy record to convey the salient points. If a more detailed rundown is required, you can always continue your commentary on the reverse side or on notes stapled to your main Contact Form.

The point is, you can now file this particular form for appropriate action, then *understand* the prospect's position at a glance 30 or 60 days later. There's no need at all to search your memory. When follow-up time does arrive, you can use your notes as a cutting edge to renew the relationship quickly. You avoid making the mistake of talking as if you've never met before.

Your Action Record:
The Anatomy of a Successful Sale

Not too many things in life are certainties, but here's one sure thing that almost any top-earning telephone pro will swear by: If you carefully track a good prospect . . . and know what action you've taken before and what action to take in the future, you'll eventually sell a large number of them.

Too many salespeople, both field reps and telephone specialists, "file" perfectly good leads in a catch-all drawer, with hopes they'll remember the leads there when the time comes to call again. Invariably, these leads are forgotten, or misplaced and fall to competitors who *do* use a system for tracking.

The simple follow-up action record on the bottom of your Contact Form is a highly effective system. (See Figure 10-4.) Every step of your relationship with a good prospect is documented in the *Action* section. You know immediately what has transpired in the past, and what has to be done in the coming days to bring a potential customer closer to the ultimate sale.

The following case dramatizes the power of keeping records on all good inquiries.

DATE	TALKED TO	COMMENTS	SEND	APP'T	CALL AGAIN	OTHER
9/15/88	A.L. LARSON	Interested (see notes)	Lit.		9/18/88	WANTS ENG. PRESENT
9/18/88	LARSON & ADAMS	OPEN FOR BID		9/30/88		
9/30/88		PRESENTATION				PROPOSAL BY 10/10/88

FOLLOW-UP ACTION RECORD

Figure 10-4

Tracking Gwinn B.'s $39,000 Phone Order

Gwinn sells phototypesetting equipment. She uses the telephone extensively to contact businesses that have (or want to acquire) the capability of doing their own typesetting. She also calls typography shops in an effort to replace existing equipment with her company's machines.

When she had been in the sales position only a few months, Gwinn observed that typesetters, as a professional group, often move from employment situations to their own shops. A person who displays above-average talent seldom remain satisfied working for someone else.

Gwinn realized that it wasn't really adequate to track just businesses; *she had to track the people within those firms.* The importance of doing this paid off quickly for her.

One day Gwinn phoned a major printing company and was connected to the Graphics Department. The saleswoman delivered her presentation to the head typesetter. During the conversation, Gwinn learned that her contact was planning to go on his own sometime in the future.

A Prospect Form was completed for the printing company and for the typesetter himself. Gwinn made notes on everything the typesetter said about what he preferred in a machine.

On follow-up calls to the company over the next year, Gwinn always made it a point to chat with the typesetter as well as with the people who purchased machines. Each contact found the typesetter a little closer to making his big move. Finally, 18 months after their initial talk, the man gave Gwinn a verbal order for her $39,000 machine!

She now tracks some 100 individuals, plus the firms they work for. Between the people who start their own businesses—and those who switch employers—Gwinn is confident that she'll get over $500,000 in sales within another year!

Tracking each prospect pays unbelievable profits down the road. So does tracking the progress of your *overall* telephone power-selling program. We'll look at how that's done next.

The Daily Call Tally Sheet: A Priceless Source of Program Statistics

Nearly every telephone selling expert periodically asks these questions:

- Am I closing as effectively as I can?
- Am I getting too many "A" prospects because I'm not qualifying stringently enough (or too few because of overly difficult qualifications)?
- Based on daily calling results, am I spending the correct amount of time on the phone?
- Do the number of "D" inquiries point to a faulty prospect list?

To come up with crystal-clear answers, a control device is required; one that provides for a recap of *daily results*. The *Daily Call Tally Sheet* (Figure 10-5) does exactly that.

DAILY CALL TALLY SHEET

Date	Total Calls Today	Presentations Today	Total Prospects	Rated			
				A	B	C	D

Figure 10-5

Each horizontal line represents one day of telephone activity. Here are step-by-step instructions for using the Tally Sheet:

DATE	— Today's date.
TOTAL CALLS TODAY	— How many times the caller actually *dialed* prospect numbers, whether they were contacted or not.
PRESENTATIONS TODAY	— Of the total number of calls attempted, how many resulted in *presentations?* (Expect about 25 to 33 percent.)
TOTAL PROSPECTS	— Of total presentations, how many can you classify as qualified prospects interested in buying? Don't count the ones that didn't pass your qualifications questions. Here, you want to count *only* the people who could conceivably buy from you now or later.
RATED **A, B, C** *AND* **D**	— This is a breakdown, *by rating,* of TOTAL PRESENTATIONS today.

You now have a simple but effective method for analyzing the progress and impact of telephoning on a day-by-day basis.

The following instance illustrates the potential value of figures like those contained in your Daily Call Tally Sheet.

How Andy R. Controls His Income: A Story of Breathtaking Growth Through Telephone Selling

Andy sells commercial building maintenance by telephone. His normal practice was to spend about two hours

contacting prospects by phone, and the balance of the day out
on personal sales visits. One fairly typical day during these
initial years in business looked like this:

DAILY CALL TALLY SHEET

Date	Total Calls Today	Presentations Today	Total Prospects	Rated			
				A	B	C	D
6-9	20	8	2	1		1	

Figure 10-6

It soon became evident to the salesman that a two-hour
stint on the telephone would yield one "A" prospect. A careful look at his closing ratios revealed that he needed three
"A" prospects for each sale. Andy had been going along at the
rate of 1½ sales per week, but he needed 3 sales a week to
meet his income objectives.

Very simply, a neat *doubling* of his telephone calling
should do the trick; four hours per day on the phone should
certainly provide two "A" prospects a day (ten a week) and
the desired 3 or so sales based on established ratios.

What actually *did* occur over the ensuing six months on
the double calling schedule astonished Andy. First, let's look
at Figure 10-7 for a typical daily breakdown on that increased schedule.

DAILY CALL TALLY SHEET

Date	Total Calls Today	Presentations Today	Total Prospects	Rated			
				A	B	C	D
2-7	46	18	6	3	1		2

Figure 10-7

Going from two to four hours a day of calling *more* than doubled his prior results! Why? Andy gave this phenomenon extensive thought and analysis. He came up with these plausible reasons for the disproportionate growth:

- Two hours on the phone meant he was just getting "warmed up" when it was time to quit. Four hours, however, allowed him time to hit maximum stride, and stay there awhile.

- As Andy spent more time calling, he rapidly grew more adept and confident.

- His "pipeline" was getting filled with strong follow-up prospects who were apt to be "A's", and thus far easier to close.

- He was getting better known by those in his market and was more readily accepted by them.

The main point is, Andy *controls* his income by merely "turning up the volume" of his telephone selling effort. And he receives a big bonus by receiving *more* than twice the results from a doubled effort.

Specialized Tracking Methods
for Building Your Telephone Sales Volume

You can adjust your calling hours to obtain precisely the level of results needed to meet or exceed a predetermined sales objective, just as Andy did. All it takes is (1) a few weeks of Daily Call data to see how many "A" prospects each hour of calling produces, and (2) an idea of how many "A's" you need to close one sale.

That's only the beginning of how the Daily Call Tally Sheet can help you. The following are a few suggestions that will guide you to tighter control of your calling program and business growth.

Watch your proportion of "hot" and "cold" leads

If you're getting too many "A" leads in comparison with "C" and "D's," and if those seemingly hot prospects are not closing as often as you feel they should, try tightening up your qualification questions. Out of, say, ten rated prospects, an expected mix would be one "A," two "B's," three "C's," and four "D's."

By the same token, an overabundance of "D's," along with a shortage of "A" prospects, could indicate that yours is an excessively rigorous qualification routine. Remember, seemingly hot leads don't help you much if they're difficult to close!

Compare your results with general averages

Whether you close by phone on the first contact, or call to qualify prospects for field sales appointments, you can use the rule of thumb, shown in Figure 10-8, to check your performance.

Of course there is plenty of latitude for variance here. An extremely high-ticket product of comparative complexity would probably *not* result in five ready to buy prospects in 20 presentations. On the other side of the coin, a newspaper

TOTAL CALLS	TOTAL PRESENTATIONS	TOTAL PROSPECTS
60	**20**	**5**

Figure 10-8

subscription could conceivably be double that of the example.

Basically, look for the ratios shown above, then establish your own performance parameters as results become visible. If your results are *significantly* different from "normal," take a hard look at the effectiveness of your presentation. If you *do* discover that you are losing sales, *find out why*. Here's a way to do it.

The "Lost Sale Report": A Positive Way to Keep Getting More Effective

A West Coast industrial supply company has a well-developed telephone sales operation that accounts for nearly 80 percent of all its volume. Yet, for all that sophistication, the firm for years had no success in one key segment of its market. And nobody in the organization had any idea why.

The Sales Manager decided to get some answers. He instituted use of a *Lost Sale Report* (Figure 10-9). One had to be completed for every fully qualified prospect who did not convert to a field appointment—and for every field appointment that did not culminate in a supply order.

In addition to generating tremendously valuable information that we'll discuss in a moment, this report *forces* both telephone people and field sales reps to take a much more careful look at *why* deals aren't materializing. It is no

LOST SALE REPORT

Company Name _____

Address _____

City _____ State _____ Zip _____

Contacts:

      Name _____ Title _____

      Name _____ Title _____

      Name _____ Title _____

Telephone _____ Ext. _____

Source of Lead _____

TELEPHONE SALES REPORT SECTION	FIELD SALES REPORT SECTION
Telephone Salesperson: _____	Field Salesperson: _____
Date Lead was Assigned: _____	Date lead was received from telephone sales: _____
Were all qualification questions asked? ☐ YES ☐ NO ☐ RATING	Date of field appointment: _____
If not, state reason: _____	Was appointment kept? ☐ YES ☐ NO
Describe why field sales appointment was not set: _____	If not, state reason: _____
If follow-up is indicated, describe planned strategy: _____	Describe why purchase was not made: _____

Figure 10-9

longer sufficient to accept a "no" and go on to the next project. Now they have to ask a prospect for reasons *why* an order isn't forthcoming.

By asking, *"Why* do you prefer Ajax Company as a supplier over us?" or, "What happened in our business relationship to make you use a different source?", many rejections started turning into orders. The simple process of *probing for reasons* opened up new fields of dialogue, and thus created renewed selling opportunities.

The *primary* objective of the Lost Sale Report was dramatically accomplished. A picture started to emerge after the Sales Manager analyzed the forms for 30 days. He immediately saw that prospects in one particular industry preferred a competitive supplier because they included two minor items in their line that our subject firm didn't offer because they considered them bothersome from a handling standpoint!

The situation was rectified, and major sales started rolling in where they didn't exist before.

Such a program control measure is definitely *not* in the exclusive domain of large corporations! Even the smallest sales organization needs to examine the reasons why customers occasionally go elsewhere. A one-man company did that and profited beyond expectation. Here's what happened.

How Fred Z. Boosted Gross
150 Percent in 40 Days

Fred Z., owner and operator of an air cargo service, built a complete telephone sales program around lost sale feedback. This is a case where all available negative feedback was used to formulate a thoroughly positive telephone sales program. The company's first attempt at selling their service to local commercial clients by telephone met with discouraging results. Fred was doing most of the calling himself, and

he was encountering points of prospect resistance that he
never ran into during face-to-face selling situations.

Still, for three more months, the boss persisted in taking the same approach he had always used with acceptable
success in past years. Finally Fred realized that he needed a
drastically different presentation to salvage his telephone
effort.

The first step was an appraisal of what had gone wrong.
All past prospect cards deemed "cold" were reviewed for
comments; most of the notes reflected various reasons why
there was no interest in Fred's cargo service. These were
compiled, then listed by frequency of occurrence.

Of the several objections that had been recorded, these
two led the "most-often-encountered" list:

- Potential buyers appeared to be extremely service
  conscious. Yet, Fred's telephone dialogue included
  nothing of substance about service.
- There appeared to be a credibility gap. Prospects
  were asking an excessive number of questions about
  Fred's company; where it was located, how long it
  had been operating, and so forth. This seemed to
  indicate doubt about the very *substance* of the firm.

Fred scrapped his prior presentation and proceeded to
build one that included strong points designed to settle prospect doubt early in the sales relationship. Immediately after
the introduction, Fred inserted the following two brief
paragraphs that he hoped would establish credibility for his
company and its service capability:

> ". . . We're not the biggest cargo service, but
> our long-term clients include many of the firms in
> your area. Most of the time, we can respond faster
> than the 'giants' and provide other services they
> can't or won't give you.

> "For the past eight years, we've really concen-
> trated on building total confidence among our cli-

ents. Now we're big enough to extend that kind of
service to a limited number of new customers."

The results were gratifying. Fred's strategy of *directly
attacking* the most prominent lost sale reasons worked bril-
liantly. In fact it was so successful that he used the new
presentation on all lost sales going back six months. That
brings us to Chapter 11, on effective follow-up procedures.

a foolproof telephone follow-up system that automatically builds a backlog of new sales 11

$\mathbf{A}$ food distributor recognizes the need for additional warehouse shelf space. The General Manager of the firm is given the responsibility of investigating various storage systems. He calls Ajax Expandable Wall Co., along with two competitive warehouse design companies, for information.

You are the regional salesperson for Ajax. You receive the inquiry, send out a brochure as promised, then contact the distribution firm later the same day.

Your call gets you nowhere fast, and your competitors encounter the same resistance. But instead of scheduling the prospect for a follow-up call down the line as *you* do, they bury this lead in a shoe box on a dusty shelf. Despite the General Manager's initial rebuff, you plan to call again in 60 days.

Here's what is taking place behind the scene.

A partner of the food distribution company is convinced of the need for more storage capacity. The General Manager, however, is opposed to the idea for reasons of his own, and makes sure the partner doesn't get too close to the positive facts the various vendors can supply. Therefore, as long as the General Manager is the contact in this firm, *nobody* will sell them a storage system.

Six weeks later, the General Manager is reassigned to other duties in the company. Two weeks after that, you follow-up as scheduled . . . fully expecting the same rejection you experienced initially. But now the *partner* takes your call, and a few days later *you have a sale in the works!*

The moral? Situations, attitudes, needs, and *people* constantly shift in most markets. Conditions ebb and flow on a daily basis. An apparently hopeless picture today can change into an ideal opportunity tomorrow, next week, next month, or next year. Methodical telephone follow-ups will get you those emerging sales opportunities!

Step-By-Step Instructions for a Model Telephone Follow-Up System

How do you effectively track leads so you know when to call back? When you consider that inquiries can arrive every time the mail is delivered, the number of required follow-ups can get out of hand quickly . . . unless you *design* a system to organize and simplify the entire process.

The last thing you need is an elaborate bookkeeping system for tracking follow-ups. The clerical time involved can seriously impede your valuable selling time. Here's a proven method that will take just a few minutes to set up and very little effort to maintain on a daily basis. Your *Prospect Forms* can be used in conjunction with an ordinary three-ring binder, organized as shown in Figure 11-1.

Prospect Forms are divided into the basic categories of "Hot," "Warm," and "Tepid." Use color-coded divider pages for each of these three sections. Next, subdivide these basic classifications in the following way.

Hot inquiries (red divider)

In back of this heading, insert tab pages identified 1 to 31; in other words, a divider for each day of the month.

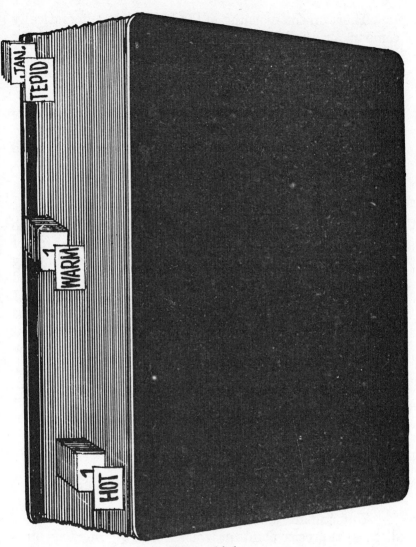

Figure 11-1

Since "Hot" leads will almost always be called back within a month, this system is ideal. For example, Ace Corporation inquires, and you rate them "A" after qualifying. A key person is out of town, so you schedule a follow-up call for the 10th of the month by inserting Ace's Prospect Form in back of Tab Page 10 in the "Hot" section.

Then, on the morning of the 10th, they automatically come up for a call-back since you check your follow-up book on a daily basis.

Warm inquiries (yellow divider)

You can use this section for "B" and "C" leads. Here again, utilize a 1 to 31 Tab Page set for scheduling follow-ups. Any lead that requires a call-back further down the road can go into your "Tepid" section.

Tepid inquiries (green divider)

This section is subdivided by *month*. Use a set of Tab Pages identified JAN. through DEC. There is no need to slot these leads for a specific day of the month for the following reason: On the 1st of each month, take the call-backs slotted for that month and distribute them evenly throughout the 1 to 31 section in the "Warm" category. That way, each will be contacted by you within the next 31 days. This is sufficient because "Tepids" are not usually so time-sensitive, and distributing them evenly balances your daily workload.

In actual practice, a follow-up system like this coordinates perfectly with almost any type of daily schedule. All it takes is a quick peek once a day to totally control your vital follow-up calls.

How Many Call-Backs Does It Take?

Unfortunately, there are no hard and fast rules that dictate the precise points at which a fully qualified appointment or sale will result along the follow-up path. There are, however, a few widely accepted guidelines:

- In one heavy equipment manufacturing company, the salespeople unanimously agree that it takes an average of seven phone calls and four personal visits to obtain a sale.

- A firm selling high-ticket intangibles has plotted the average time to close at 94 days from initial contact.
- In contrast to the above examples, a service company knows that their typical "A" lead closes in 8 days, and a valid "B" closes in just 14 days.

The point is, *telephone follow-up produces the REAL dollar* revenues. Anyone can "high-spot" expensive advertising responses or cold calls and come up with a sale now and then; it's a matter of playing the percentages. But tenacious telephone call-back activity will fill your personal sales pipeline with budding prospects at various stages of "ripeness" or readiness-to-buy. This jam-packed pipeline begins to generate orders that usually dwarf the few inevitable prospects who are presold and don't require follow-up.

This book can't provide you a "pat" formula about how much effort it will take to close your follow-up prospects. That depends on too many variables unique to your business. But you *can* find that answer by tracking call-backs through the control forms described earlier.

The real issue is. . . patience and perseverance are the virtues that separate the big earners from all the others! The following incident is a case in point.

Prioritizing: Darren T.'s "Second Attack" Strategy

One chaotic week convinced Darren of the need for an organized follow-up system based on prioritizing leads. He sells equipment related to the building industry.

On Monday, he received two calls from companies asking about machines. In addition, the advertising department handed him 12 direct mail responses, plus a note that a prior customer had referred an acquaintance with a need for equipment. By day's end, Darren contacted all 15 leads by telephone, and set appointments with 10 of them.

The next day, he got 8 more leads and managed to arrange another 6 appointments. The trouble was, a few of the prospects who sounded like very strong buying candidates had to be scheduled beyond two weeks later because of Darren's growing workload! Wednesday brought more of the same, and on it went for the rest of the week.

When the dust finally settled a month later, the salesman *did* have a few orders to show for his hectic pace, but he was sure that at least two—and perhaps as many as five— legitimate buyers slipped away to competitors because of his tardiness in getting to them. This was especially aggravating since many of the personal visits he made were to "B" and "C" prospects he could have easily put off.

Today, Darren meticulously rates each lead during the initial call, and sets the date and time of his field appointment based on that priority rating. He is doing far better at beating competitors to the business. Equally important, the methodical follow-up system he now uses gives him the control to reach the lower priority leads as time permits, and guides him along a planned call-back route that squeezes every available profit dollar out of follow-up activity.

Setting Up an Aggressive Timetable for Telephone Follow-Up

If a qualified prospect tells you to wait 90 days before getting back in touch, do you base your call-back schedule on that advice, or do you try to "read between the lines" in making your follow-up more timely?

A successful insurance agent was in the practice of taking a potential client's advice literally; he found it was costing sales. "Call me back in two months," this salesman learned, was often a gut-level guess as to how long it would take to clear up various complications. When the insurance man started *probing,* he discovered that most call-backs could be made much sooner than suggested by the prospect.

For example, the person on the other end of the line might say, "I have to get a new will completed before we discuss my insurance needs. Call me in September." A smart probe would be, "When are you seeing your attorney?" If the answer is mid-August, our man makes it a point to follow-up on August 20th.

Quarterly budgets, management changes, vacation schedules, and other factors also impact follow-up dates. If you are aware of the reason why action has to be deferred —and you are cognizant of the time considerations —you can make far more money through telephone calling!

Each case has to be evaluated individually. Sometimes you'll accept it when a potential buyer tells you to wait three months before calling again. This is largely a matter of personal credibility. *But it does pay to probe* rather than to agree passively with an arbitrary prospect-suggested follow-up date!

A strategically selected call-back date is one-half the groundwork involved in a money-making telephone follow-up program. The other vital half is described next.

Key Facts That Make
Your Follow-Up Calls Work!

There are actually *two* basic types of call-backs:

- A situation where your prospect is interested in buying, but describes some kind of obstacle that will be overcome in time, such as talking to others in the company.

- Or, your prospect does not say much to reveal interest level, but you sense that a later call is apt to be fruitful.

In either case, the caller has to quickly rekindle interest on the part of the prospect. It must be assumed that there is no recollection whatsoever of the initial telephone conversation. If the caller approaches this important second call as if there was *no* prior relationship, he or she is right back on square one in terms of rapport-building.

The fastest and most logical way to stimulate a prospect's recall of the earlier telephone conversation is to bring up *key facts* that were uncovered during the first contact; ones that are not known to just any outsider.

In any developing relationship between two people, each new conversation should begin at starting points that progress successively further into more personal topics. It would be abnormal indeed to hear a couple of long-term acquaintances greet each other with the same small formalities that near strangers use!

Your call-back should be just a bit warmer and more personal than the first discussion was. Some trust should have been established, and that trust *must* be reflected in both your choice of words, and particularly in your selection of topics. Taking good notes during your first contact will help here.

Here are specific ways to speedily reestablish that priceless rapport which may have been forgotten by your prospect.

"Reentry" Techniques: Powerful Pretexts for Renewing Telephone Sales Relationships

To illustrate the impact of making salient comments in call-backs, take a situation where you are following up three weeks after the initial contact was made. Rather than starting all over with the comparatively formal introduction prescribed in your presentation, you are able to approach the prospect this way after you reintroduce yourself:

> ". . . You may recall we discussed a new riveter for the construction jobs you have coming up next June. You mentioned certain specifications, and I took the liberty of getting a few details about that which might be interesting to you."

By bringing up specific points about the prospect's needs in this way, you reenter the relationship with tremendous power. On the other hand, a weak follow-up approach might sound like this:

> "We talked about your inquiry regarding a riveting machine, remember?"

Sad to say, the latter reentry is all too commonly used, and is hopelessly flat. It deserves prospect rejection!

Another way to quickly reestablish rapport is to lead with a nonbusiness topic. Two recent firing-line cases are:

- During one initial sales call, the prospect revealed that he had just purchased a home. At follow-up time, the caller led by asking how he liked the new house.

- A marketing department prospect mentioned to the seller that his company was soon to hold company-wide staff meetings in Hawaii. Here, the caller reentered by asking how the meetings went.

In both instances, at least five minutes of fond commentary came from the prospect, and rapport was recaptured in no uncertain terms.

Another reentry idea is to bring up industry news. If you follow newspaper financial pages and business publications, you'll invariably come upon articles pertinent to a particular prospect's sphere of operations. If the news is significant, your contact probably knows all about it, but you can always comment about it and be reasonably certain of getting a response. (Try to avoid industry news of a negative nature.)

An outstanding ad agency account executive does intensive follow-up calling. She always makes sure that plenty of data is on-hand for strong reentries.

How Thorough Documentation Keeps Judy N. Prosperous

During every initial telephone sales call she makes, Judy writes constantly. Her Prospect Form is usually covered with notes, front and back. In fact, she frequently has to staple additional sheets of paper to the original by the time she has written down all her recollections about one initial telephone conversation. Some of her cohorts feel that these extensive rundowns are overkill, but Judy is convinced that highly detailed observations are the main reason why she's a leading earner.

The practical implications of possessing lots of facts about a prospect are these:

● During follow-up, nearly every topic that comes up can be made to seem more important if the caller adds appropriate personal or "inside" information.

For example:

Prospect: "We should be ready to start laying the groundwork for this project as soon as we get our new manager trained."

Caller: "Yes . . . I recall you mentioning that a new customer service manager would be joining your firm. If you think it would help, we can provide an hour or two of special familiarization as part of our service to you."

● If your prospect gets the feeling that you are aware of goings-on in his or her company (as the above example conveys), there is less likelihood that phony excuses will be used to put you off.

Every caller will eventually zero in on a level of note-taking that is personally suitable. You may decide to record extensive notes about a conversation as Judy does—go to the other extreme with a few cryptic comments on key issues or settle at a point somewhere in the middle. *The important thing is to document sufficient facts to make your reentry calls as potent as you can.*

Here are a few other ideas to make your follow-up calls more profitable.

A List of Crucial "Dos" and "Don'ts" from Herman V.— An Acknowledged Telephone Sales Expert

Starting with one small office and a tiny store room for a modest inventory of products, Herman built his graphics supply business into one of the largest in a West Coast city. He accomplished it through a combined direct mail and telephone sales effort that he executed himself for three years.

Today, there are five well-trained callers on Herman's staff, backed up by a sophisticated computer inquiry-handling system. The 25-employee operation is now housed in a 4,000 square foot building.

If anyone can speak with authority on effective telephone technique, it's this man. He has set up rather rigid guidelines for his callers to follow. Some of the "dos" and "don'ts" he believes most strongly in pertain to call-back procedures. Here are the key ones:

• **DO** make call-backs exactly when promised. True, sometimes you won't specify a date and time for various reasons, but whenever you *do,* by all means adhere to that commitment! Herman feels that this kind of punctuality helps build credibility and an image of reliability.

• **DO** make sure at some point during the follow-up call that your prospect's circumstances are still favorable. He or she may proceed down the path with you, unaware that subtle changes in the situation have made your product or service unsuitable.

Check qualifications again, and make certain they are still substantially in line with your requirements. It'll save time.

• **DON'T** let frustration reflect in your voice if you are put off again. As difficult as it might be, remain gracious at all times. Herman is convinced that even the slightest trace of caller exasperation will be projected to the ears of your prospect and will impair the relationship. If it takes a third, a fourth, or even a fifth call-back, so be it.

● **DON'T** assume that your contact still recalls vital details about your product or service. As the follow-up call progresses, reiterate key features and benefits that have probably been forgotten by your prospect during the time elapsed since the initial conversation. There is nothing so embarrassing as getting down to the close, and having your contact ask questions about fundamentals.

Follow-up telephone calls are usually associated with the ongoing cultivation of a relatively stable prospect and customer base. But there *are* telephone sales campaigns that are essentially "one-shot." Chapter 12 explores these.

teleblitz:
an extraordinary
telephone approach for
building major sales 12

$\mathbf{A}$ nationally renowned advertising man says: "The fastest way to kill a bad product is to do great advertising for it." In illuminating that statement, this leader told of a professional sports organization that spent a fortune attracting people to see their mediocre team play. They *did* fill most of the available seats in the stadium, but most ticket buyers knew they had been conned.

A *Teleblitz* zone saturation calling campaign will almost always bring astonishing sales results, but the long-range success of a company really depends on the quality, usefulness, and general acceptance of its product or service.

We are assuming in this discussion that the subject is some tangible or intangible item that *does have a clearly established niche in a defined market . . . and is a legitimate value of acceptable quality.*

With those basic prerequisites in place, we can proceed to explore a way to gain remarkable sales success quickly.

Teleblitz is a telephone calling campaign conducted on a zone saturation basis. It differs from a traditional marketing program in the following ways:

179

- Teleblitz demands a high volume of calls; 50 to 60 a day per caller, or more.

- Several callers may be used, rather than the one or two present in typical programs. A staff numbering five to ten or more people is not uncommon in zone saturation.

- The presentation utilized in Teleblitz is brief and right to the point. The objective of such a campaign is fast, wide exposure, so the subtle persuasive strategies are largely set aside in order to increase *total* contact.

- As mentioned earlier, follow-up is often *not* a factor in Teleblitz because of the extreme control complications involved. Thus, the entire recordkeeping process is purposely simplified in such a large-scale effort.

- Zone saturation is utilized almost exclusively in cold-calling. The only conceivable situation where prior leads are called would be when a company has obtained hundreds or thousands of inquiries from a trade show or from some especially productive advertising program.

There are scores of valid applications for Teleblitz zone saturation. Here are a few you'll eventually encounter.

Three Extra-Rich Markets George H. Taps Through Saturation Calling

As a telephone sales consultant, George H. is exposed to an endless variety of program requirements and objectives. He deals with companies ranging from direct-to-consumer marketers to major industrial corporations. He has occasion to prescribe Teleblitz for certain needs. Here are a few of them:

A cosmetics manufacturer sells direct-to-consumers through mail order. This one-dimensional approach had always seemed adequate, but the company wanted a concrete reading on what the market potential would be if telephone contact was added as a backup punch.

George obtained ordinary telephone directories covering a four-county area near a large midwest city. A mailing was sent, then a telephone room was set up at company headquarters. A 30-day test then commenced.

Nearly 60 percent of the list was covered in the allocated time. The calling produced $29,000 in cash sales over and above normal expectations. Teleblitz is now a permanent component in the company's sales operation.

A printed circuit manufacturer was planning a new product introduction. The objective was to reach a pre-profiled market *quickly*—before aggressive competitors could react. Trade magazine media ads, the traditional method of getting the word out, would definitely *not* achieve the desired results.

George recruited ten electronic engineering students from a nearby university and had the entire list covered by calls within 16 days. *Exceptional* market penetration was attained through this Teleblitz program.

A truck rental company simply was not getting satisfactory business out of a sizeable city near its location. Ads and mailers were not getting response here. George obtained lists based on *known* renter characteristics and put four callers on the phones with a simple presentation. Within 60 days, this stubborn territory was producing a record number of rental agreements.

The consultant can cite numerous examples of Teleblitz boosting sales in lagging territories. But the most exciting programs to him are new product introductions. Zone saturation calling can economically get big sales numbers at *extremely low marketing costs.* George does insist, however,

that one of the keys to success in large-scale calling is the
quality of the list used.

Finding a Virtually Endless Source of Qualified Buyers Through Profiling

There is nothing more unproductive than trying to
make a sale where a built-in need or interest does not exist.
That's *exactly* what happens when off-target lists are used
for calling or direct mail. This phenomenon is captured perfectly in the old saying, "trying to sell ice cubes to Eskimos."

Today, there are countless sources of lists. Businesses
are identified in terms of S.I.C. (Standard Industrial Clas-
sification) category, which describes the kind of activities
they are engaged in. Commercial enterprises can be further
qualified by number of employees, annual dollar sales, size
of ad budget, and so forth.

Consumers, too, can be nicely classified. There are lists
of mail order buyers, business opportunity seekers, leisure
time spenders, and many more.

While many Teleblitz campaigns rely on pure call volume and do not attempt to zero in on a qualified market, the
most cost-effective programs *do* include certain steps to
pre-profile a target audience. To illustrate the basic process
of profiling, let's look at the steps George took in setting up
the previously described Teleblitz programs.

In the direct-to-consumer cosmetics program, George
went only as far as studying basic demographics of the coun
ties earmarked for calling. The feature he wanted was a
middle-class population, with women most apt to purchase
fragrances by telephone. Upper classes preferred to buy in
department stores, and lower economic levels did not usually
possess sufficient disposable income to make such a purchase.

This category also yielded the largest *identifiable audience* in the test zone.

In the printed circuit Teleblitz project, pinpointing the audience was simple. Calls would be made to *known users* of machines that accommodated the new product. A widely read electronics trade publication was able to supply a list of these users that was alleged to be 80 percent accurate. The list was expensive, but a bargain in terms of the time-saving it brought to the calling effort.

In the truck rental calling program, George faced a task of compiling a list of prospects. From company sales history, he *knew* the categories of companies likely to rent trucks. It was then a matter of finding out which ones existed in the target city.

The consultant selected such classifications as movers, haulers, heavy product retailers and manufacturers, major service stations, and a few others. Then he combed the following sources:

- Chamber of Commerce business directory
- Classified telephone directory
- Ads placed in recent area newspapers
- Two mailing lists of businesses in the city's zip code areas

The result was a list of some 400 establishments that appeared to be candidates. This, George guessed, was about 90 percent of the total potential.

When you have your target market all lined up, you are ready to build a special Teleblitz phone presentation. Here's how some of the pros do it.

Designing a Short-Form Pitch That Works

Keep in mind that *exposure* is the primary objective in a Teleblitz calling campaign. *A large number of contacts* is expected to more than compensate for the elimination of sales strategies.

The first element you can drop is your *qualification questions*. Since Teleblitz calls are almost always made to a cold list, there is very little use in finding out if your contact *can* buy. It makes more sense to simply *close* and find out *that* way!

Let's examine that for just a moment longer. If you are faced with the task of sifting through advertising leads in order to develop qualified prospects for a field sales organization, you have to qualify thoroughly. But cold-calling a big list requires *coarse* screening in the interest of saving time. If that coarse screening reveals interest, you can proceed in one of these directions, depending on the nature of your selling method:

- If the prospect is to be referred to a field salesperson, you can more tightly qualify *after* the coarse screening.

- If you can consummate the sale during the initial telephone contact, go for the close either right after the coarse screening, or in place of it.

The second major difference in a Teleblitz pitch is its emphasis on satisfaction, and its corresponding de-emphasis on product description. It stands to reason that the person receiving a comparatively to-the-point call will be somewhat wary; the seller is proceeding with a brief presentation—delivered at high daily volume—and must be careful not to convey pressure. Because of this, the following points have to be built-in:

- If prospect consent is given, it is understood that there is *no* obligation to buy if a field sales visit is involved.

- If a telephone close is involved, the prospect must be reassured that cancellation, exchange, or return is perfectly permissible within a reasonable time after delivery.

Figure 12-1 shows a typical logic diagram for a Teleblitz presentation.

Logic Flow and Dialogue Suggestions for an Effective Teleblitz Presentation

The brief presentation shown in Figure 12-1 is used by an insurance agency to set appointments for field salespeople. The entire process normally consumes three to four minutes if delivered from start to finish. It is comprised of this general dialogue:

1. *Introduction*

"Hello . . . this is _____ of _____ insurance agency."

2. *Coarse screen*

"Have you been thinking about major medical coverage?" ("No" response is further probed with, "Would you be interested in finding out more about our coverage package?" Another "No" terminates the call. A "Yes" to either the coarse screen or the probe leads to the following qualification questions.)

3. *Tighter qualifications*

- "Do you carry major medical now?" (Determine if group plan, or other type)
- Find out general family health situation, number of people to be covered, and ages.

  (If indications are that this is a buying candidate, proceed to Step 4.)

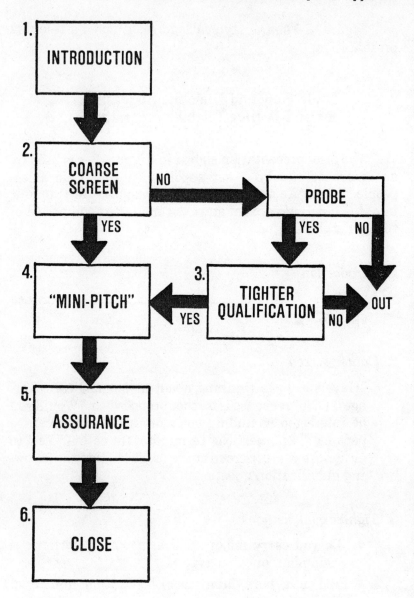

Figure 12-1

4. Mini-pitch

"We're one of the oldest and most respected companies in America. Our special family plan provides excellent coverage for groups like yours, at extremely competitive rates." (Go directly to the Assurance Step.)

5. Assurance

"There is absolutely *no* obligation for finding out the details. We have hundreds of policyholders in the area, and all of them can vouch for the way we deal with clients.
(Go directly to Close.)

6. Close

"Mr. _____ will be seeing people in your neighborhood _____ evening. If everyone will be home then, I can have him drop over at _____."

Note that a short-form Teleblitz presentation does not accommodate much prospect response. Except for the coarse screening and possible additional qualification steps, it is pretty much one-sided, with the seller doing most of the talking. There are obvious shortcomings in this approach, but the advantage of *control* outweighs the negatives. Asking for prospect statements will invariably cost precious time—and open the discussion to extensive wandering.

A saleswoman in a big ticket business uses a brief pitch similar to the one described above, and has added an interesting dimension to her telephone sales program.

Paula Z. Gets Startling Results
Through the Zone Saturation System

Paula sets up field appointments for a swimming pool construction company in a southern city. She came upon a system that gets magnified results for Teleblitz calling.

When the woman first started with the company, she more or less randomly selected residential neighborhoods as targets for telephone solicitation. The results were unspectacular and consistent. She came upon a successful new formula quite accidentally.

A recent swimming pool buyer asked the company's field salesperson to call a neighbor he knew had expressed interest in building a pool. The salesperson contacted the prospect directly, successfully closed a pool contract, then mentioned the sequence of events to Paula.

It didn't take long for the woman to realize that by concentrating on neighborhoods that already *had* homes with her company's pools, she could probably maximize calling results. So Paula acquired a list of successfully installed projects, then compiled the names and phone numbers of residents within a three-block radius of those completed pools.

Paula designed a short-form telephone pitch that basically embodied these points:

- The nearby home with the new pool had essentially the same property dimensions as the prospect's. Since the pool worked into the available land very nicely for *that* house, it certainly would for the prospect's.

- It was known that a certain real estate appreciation had already been realized by the pool owner. Since that house was generally comparable to the prospect's, the potential gain to the prospect could be estimated with reasonable accuracy.

- The prospect, if truly serious about a pool purchase, could call the neighborhood pool owner to check on the quality of the installation. (This was an effective bit of merchandising. Prior permission was received from most pool owners; if they agreed to accept these reference calls, the company provided a supply of free chemicals for their trouble.)

As you can imagine, Paula's zone saturation calls now hit the mark with much more impact. Her argument *directly touches on benefits that each prospect can identify with*. The immediate result shows a 40 percent boost in the number of qualified field sale visits!

A distributor of educational films took its *local* Teleblitz sales success and turned it into a *nationwide* profit machine.

"Cloning" to Multiply Sales

Once a simple, short-form telephone presentation has been perfected, the only thing stopping a vastly expanded program is people-power. If one caller generates $5,000 a day in sales, ten callers should chalk up $50,000 a day. It can be as simple as that.

The fact is, just about every major Teleblitz operation that is now functioning on a national scale started with one or two callers. As successful methods evolved, it became glaringly evident that this "calling machine" could easily be expanded to cover more counties, states, and eventually every corner of the nation.

The answer, in a manner of speaking, is *cloning*. By coming as close as possible to *perfectly duplicating* the original successful calling apparatus, expansion proceeds smoothly and easily. Every element in the effort has to be reproduced as faithfully as possible. To reach the desired level of extended effort:

- Added callers have to possess personal characteristics that closely resemble those of the original crew.
- Facilities, such as telephone setup and calling environment, should be like the beginning system and space, enlarged to handle the growing capability.

The vital point is to *avoid altering a successful approach*. Stay with the combination that you know works. You will very probably discover certain characteristics in callers that suit them especially well for selling your product or service. By all means stay with the people who demonstrate those strengths.

The following pages provide valuable guidelines for finding, evaluating, and hiring callers for both Teleblitz programs and the more traditional telephone sales positions.

Essential Steps for Finding and Recruiting Good Callers

While there are widely varying beliefs and practices applied in the realm of recruiting, the following basics are recommended when *callers* are the subject of a search. These guidelines are particularly important when you have to locate a number of competent people to staff a large-scale Teleblitz program.

● *Classified help-wanted ads,* usually a very effective way to attract applicants, should be *straightforward* in expressing the nature of the responsibilities. Some companies try to glorify the position and succeed only in misleading the applicants. Come right out and say that the job involves four, six, or eight hours of calling—or whatever else the responsibilities entail.

● Whether your ad invites a call from interested applicants, or requests a mailed résumé, be sure you have at least one opportunity to hear the person over the telephone. Experienced recruiters are perpetually amazed at how different an in-person voice can be from the way it sounds via electronic communication. You want to know how your *potential customers* will hear a particular voice!

● *Check references!* Many, many employers never take the trouble, and run into problems they could easily have avoided. If an otherwise delightful and qualified person chronically antagonizes others, it helps to be aware of that problem as early as possible.

● *Ask the people you hire if they have friends who are available for calling jobs.* Professional callers often have acquaintances in the field who are looking for work. Several firms heavily into major Teleblitz programs use this technique and *rarely* have to place ads for people!

In addition to those fundamental hiring guidelines, the personal *characteristics* of the person you consider for a calling job is of overriding importance! Telephone sales experts pretty much agree that certain inherent traits have to be present in a strong calling candidate. Here's how one outstanding manager rates applicants.

Mark V.'s Grading System for Identifying Effective Telephone Salespeople

Mark V. is responsible for staffing major calling operations such as political campaigns, newspaper subscription drives, fund raising efforts, and so forth. Over the years, he has devised a grading system for evaluating potential telephone salespeople.

This recruiter knows that a good caller will possess a basic set of personality characteristics that usually combine to make a winner. Therefore, before Mark will hire a particular person, he or she must have many favorable traits.

Mark readily admits he'd never be as fortunate as to find *all* the important traits in one person, but he does insist on a score of 70 percent. Each of the characteristics, listed below, gets 7.7 points.

As he conducts an interview, a trait is checked off the moment he perceives it. The total checked is multiplied by 7.7, and hopefully a 70 or better is the aggregate. Here is Mark's checklist, not necessarily in order of relative importance:

1. Enunciates clearly. Has good speaking voice. Is able to project personality.

2. Puts "punch" into speech. Uses exciting language instinctively.

3. Gets to the point quickly. Doesn't ramble.

4. Has empathy and sensitivity.

5. Is a good listener. *Never* cuts in when you are speaking.

6. Is genuinely people-oriented and gregarious.

7. Doesn't seem to be excessively vulnerable to rejection.

8. Has above-average intelligence. Improvises quickly.

9. *Wants* to sell by telephone. Is enthusiastic.

10. Seems well-organized, appears to have good work habits.

11. Has a high energy level, but not overly tempermental.

12. Has some background in the industry where calling will be conducted. Knows some of the "buzzwords."

13. Doesn't mind starting work very early in the morning (especially critical if a West Coast caller has to reach eastern-based prospects).

Your Teleblitz presentation is ready, your market has been profiled, and your callers have been selected. The next step is a national calling effort. The big question that comes now is this: *How do you keep long-distance telephone expenses down to manageable levels in a large-scale telephone calling program?*

Controlling Expenses for
Nationwide Calling Campaigns

There *are* alternatives today in long-distance calling. Several independent phone service companies provide services that may save you some important money on your monthly phone bill. Each of these firms offers different arrangements to residential users and businesses, so you have to find out how the various services work in your area.

Some considerations when you select a long distance company include:

- having the company compare their charges to a recent bill from the company providing your current service.
- how long the company has been in business.
- ensuring that the company has a local service office in your area.
- talking to local users of the service you are considering.

In the past, there has been some criticism of the voice transmission quality obtained through alternative telephone networks. Look into this *carefully*, since effective telephone selling is not compatible with static or other problems. Ask to talk to other subscribers to the service and find out if they encounter transmission difficulties.

While these companies still have problems here and there, it is significant to cut up to 50 percent off of a monthly telephone bill. And these services are certain to remain on a strong upgrade in the future. Check your classified telephone directory and get the details if one or more are operating in your vicinity.

Here are a few more very good ways to keep telephone costs within reasonable limits.

Five Important Ways to Slash
Your Mass Calling Telephone Costs

In most states, you can plug rented or purchased telephone equipment into your phone jack—the same way you plug a lamp into an electrical outlet.

De-regulation of America's $53 billion telephone industry has created fertile ground for firms in competition with the giant utilities. These organizations, sometimes known as "interconnect" companies, differ from the long-distance alternative firms described earlier because they are primarily in the telephone *equipment* business.

The de-regulation, mentioned above, means that the telephone charges you are accustomed to seeing from utilities have been separated from their equipment and service costs. In theory, that means you can plug your own bargain telephone into established big-utility lines and pay a nominal price for that privilege. Depending on where you live, and how good a deal you can get on equipment, the savings can indeed be significant.

If you *do* decide to shop for your own telephone at one of the many independent manufacturing firms in that growing new business, check these details *carefully* before you actually make the investment:

1. Find out from your local telephone company how much they'll charge to install your equipment, and what the monthly fee is for using their lines.

2. Get *definite* information from the independent telephone supplier about their maintenance capability, and what it will cost for service. Your local utility will *not* service equipment you purchase from a competitor!

3. Be sure the telephone you like is a type that is Federal Communications Commission (FCC)-approved. In fact, be meticulous about observing *all* the regulations involved in using interconnect equipment.

Here are four other tips for dramatically reducing your heavy-volume calling expenses:

● Unless it's an absolute necessity for some reason, *avoid* making long-distance calls on a person-to-person basis! Such operator-assisted calls are extremely expensive.

● The same thing is true when you use a telephone company credit card or reverse the charges. These are also operator-assisted, and go at a premium rate that really adds up on your monthly bill. Make your calls dial direct *station-to-station* in order to save up to 54 percent under "person" rates.

● If possible, call during "off" hours. For example, a 5 p.m. to 11 p.m. station call might save you as much as 70 percent under daytime person rates.

● Talk a bit faster, and keep it as brief as you can without cutting the heart and soul out of your presentation. A few seconds here and there will always add up to a considerable monthly sum.

In many sales organizations, *incoming* calls are as important as outgoing contacts and must be made easy for the prospect. Here is today's best way to make it easy.

Using Toll-Free Phone Service to Boost Prospect Response

The toll-free 800 number is an awesomely powerful sales tool that is certain to influence *your* business in some way in the not-too-distant future. This relatively new selling medium lends itself especially well to magazine or newspaper ads, direct mail, catalog sales, and radio or TV promotions.

An 800 number is actually an *incoming* WATS (Wide Area Telephone Service) line that enables your prospects to call orders into you from any part of the country at no cost to the purchaser. A buyer simply dials 800, followed by your number, to make the toll-free call. This rapidly growing electronic marketing technique is particularly effective when applied to the following tasks:

● *Making a direct sale.* The buyer responds to your advertising and uses the 800 number to place an order. Payment arrangements can be via credit card charge or C.O.D.

● *Dealer referral.* If your product or service is high-ticket and doesn't lend itself to a close by telephone, the 800 number is used to steer the prospect to a nearby dealer who can cultivate the sale.

● *Lead generation.* Ads for a comparatively complex product or service can advise a prospect to call on the 800 line to obtain more information, such as product sheets or brochures. The inquiry is later followed up by an *outgoing* telephone call.

As with the alternative long-distance telephone companies discussed a bit earlier, there are a number of firms offering incoming WATS service. These companies are also equipped to handle the incoming calls for subscribers.

An 800 number setup makes tremendous sense for companies using nationwide advertising propelled by hefty budgets. If you aren't big enough to consider it right now, keep it in mind for the time when you *are*. The increasing reluctance of consumers to venture out on shopping trips will accelerate 800 number use.

On that note, let's explore the intriguing possibility of your own telephone sales consulting business. When you have achieved reasonable experience in designing and conducting calling programs, there are an endless number of clients who will want your guidance.

multiply your income with a telephone sales business of your own 13

This book is devoted to topics eagerly sought by many companies now involved—or just getting involved—in selling by telephone. Backed by reasonable experience that would further deepen your understanding of the prescribed methods and techniques, this information most certainly represents a body of knowledge that you can successfully sell to firms of all descriptions.

Qualifications You Should Have to Make Your Own Business Work

The needs in industry are tremendously diverse. One firm may need only a Teleblitz program to qualify a heavy quantity of trade show leads. Another may want to deliver everything from product presentations to custom in-house seminars for key personnel. One consulting assignment may run just four hours, the next one six months.

Each organization will be at a different stage of sophistication in the evolution of its telephone effort. Each will have different internal capabilities and available time to accomplish its own program development. You will often contribute just in areas where outside assistance is required.

The existence of opportunity is definitely *not* the problem. The major decision you face is this: Do you have the *temperament* to go out and teach others to be skillful in selling by telephone? Will you be content to have the front-line action to become a behind-the-scenes advisor?

Both are questions only *you* can answer. In addition to those self-judgments, here are a few basic points you should understand before embarking on your own telephone sales enterprise:

- You should be comfortable talking to business owners and middle to upper-management people.

- You should *not be timid* when it comes to frankly expressing opinions about situations you perceive in client organizations. If a particular method is used that threatens to compromise your efforts, you have to *tactfully* campaign for changes. You help *nobody* by tolerating a counterproductive environment. The key people in a client company *want* to know where the snags are . . . and depend on a consultant to tell them!

- You have to be willing to monitor a client's program until you are reasonably sure it's well on the way to success. This may require an investment of your time at reduced pay—after the primary work has been done. It pays off handsomely in satisfied clients.

Here's another area that will demand a major allocation of your time.

Modularizing Your Own Business

Let's say a potential client company has proceeded down the path in building a telephone sales department. The process goes smoothly until the company reaches a certain point. The presentation has been completed, the objectives are defined, space is set aside—even the callers have been obtained. But *implementation* is the roadblock. Getting the "wheels" to turn properly is a hangup for this company, so you are called to lend assistance.

In this situation and similar ones, you can be *totally* effective if you have the ability to lay out quickly a *pre-established* implementation plan. It's a series of steps precisely engineered to orchestrate the various components of a program and set them into coordinated motion. To repeat:

> *The specific aspect of a program that you may be called upon to deliver has been worked out in advance, and is ready for use exactly when the need arises.*

A self-employed consultant who does *not* modularize and package a program this way will usually be as lost as the client until the problems are all examined and worked out. That consumes valuable time, and sometimes even destroys the credibility and image of competence a consultant has worked hard to build.

Some would argue that *every* client problem requires new solutions. But really, that's just like reinventing the wheel. While it *is* true that the standard formulas you have in a particular module have to be *adjusted* to fit a certain client's situation, all those problems are basically identical. Why waste time doing them over and over?

Client confidence is another issue, touched on earlier. If the marketing people came to you for help in profiling their ideal prospect, they'll feel a lot better about your ability if you can *immediately relate a progression of steps you always follow in getting the job done!* They will know at once that you rely on a carefully-worked-out method. The "play-it-by-ear" consultant can only mumble, "Okay . . . I'll work it out." Then everyone keeps their fingers crossed!

Packaging Program Components
to Fit Client Requirements

There are any number of ways to lay out the modules of your telephone sales program. The objective is *optimum flexibility*. You want the ability to fit your "pieces" neatly into a program that might be partially completed by your client.

Module 1—feasibility study

A company is intrigued by the concept of selling by telephone, but isn't sure if it will work for them. Your function . . .

is to test the market by personally calling prospects in the industry. Then, when sample results are available, you report your conclusions and recommendations.

Module 2—program planning

A company wants to proceed, but asks you to specify everything needed. Your function . . .

based on available market data, client resources and program objectives, is to prepare a detailed plan describing what's needed, and a timetable that dictates when the events will occur. Such a plan should include a rundown of all expected costs along with sales estimates.

Module 3—presentation

Your assistance is required in writing the telephone presentation. Your function . . .

is to go through the checklist (covered earlier in this book) *with the client, then prepare a presentation based on that information.*

Module 4—train callers

The client may want you to recruit people, then bring them up to speed in use of the presentation. Your function . . .

is to use a preestablished method that assures a reasonable level of skill in the selected callers. (More about how to do this a little later.)

Module 5—devise controls

Your client's Sales Manager wants a system for tracking the results of calling, and assuring that field follow-up visits are made to qualified prospects. Your function . . .

is to propose the use of the Daily Call Tally Sheet, Prospect Contact Form, Lost Sale Report, plus any other system that provides management information.

Module 6—program implementation

The client asks you to get the ball rolling. Program "kick-off" demands that all the necessary pieces are properly in place. Your function . .

is to oversee the physical actions that get things moving. It is particularly important to see that proper patterns are established at this critical stage.

Module 7—program monitoring

The busy Sales Manager now asks you to work with the callers for six months to keep the telephone sales program on-track. Your function . . .

is to work out a schedule for regular visits to the firm in order to monitor. You'll deliver frequent memos—and have periodic meetings with client management—to keep them abreast of progress.

*Plus, you'll make authorized changes and fine-tune
as needed to keep the program productive.*

Each module should have a comprehensive outline of
steps you normally take to get it done effectively. Again,
some adjustments might be necessary here and there, but
you now have a solid foundation for delivering consistent
performance!

Now that you possess a delivery formula, where can it
be sold?

Where Patti S. Finds an Endless List
of Prime Prospects for
Her Telephone Sales Expertise

Patti served as Manager of Marketing Services for an
East Coast transportation company until she decided to
strike out on her own. She decided on telephone sales consulting because such a program had been a smashing success
at her former company.

The ideal prospect base for Patti's services, as she saw
it, was actually *every* product or service company with annual gross sales between $5 million and $50 million. Her
prior firm was in that bracket, and she understood some of
the problems they encountered.

This group of potential clients was vast, and rather than
grind through the total available list, Patti preferred to
devote her attention to the *most likely buyers* of telephone
consulting services. Who were these better prospects? Patti
figured they were companies that did heavy advertising and
trade show exhibiting. It stood to reason that any aggressive
advertiser was generating lots of leads. And any time there
were many leads, there was inevitably a need to use the
telephone to reach them all.

Now, how could the heavy advertisers and trade show
displayers be quickly identified? Easy! Just check the major
trade magazines, and walk through a trade show or two and
make a list. That's *precisely* what Patti did.

The new telephone sales consultant set a high percentage of appointments with those companies classified as strong promoters. Nearly every one *did* admit to Patti a problem in the areas of inquiry control and efficient conversion of leads to sales. And these firms *all* complained about high field sales costs.

So there was abundant business. As expected, Patti found a diverse mix of companies and a wide variety of assignments that needed doing. One of her first dilemmas was how much to charge, what kind of terms to give, and how to handle other fee questions from clients.

How to Charge for Consulting Services

Setting fee levels—and taking into account *all* the services she would be asked to provide—was a major task for Patti. She was determined to avoid a situation where she might be asked a price that hadn't been carefully thought out in advance.

The consultant used the modular approach described earlier in this chapter. She put a flat rate on each module and based it on the estimated time it would take to complete the task. Although there are numerous ways to arrive at a rate structure, Patti used the following reasoning to establish a rate structure with which she was most comfortable.

Her last salary as an employee broke down to about $10 per hour. Since she felt ready for an increase (and was sure her talent justified it), Patti decided to calculate from a basic hourly rate of $20. That was merely the first step in her formula.

Next, Patti considered the time entailed in acquiring clients. If she was able to actually *work* 40 hours a week at the $20 rate, it would give her $800 gross per week compared to the $400 she earned as an employee. Nice on the surface of it...*but how many hours (without pay) would it take to get one hour of consulting work?* Patti figured one hour. Therefore, to even hope of reaching an income higher than her old salary, Patti set her consulting rate at $35 per hour.

As an example of how that rate equated to the cost of a module, let's take the preparation of a telephone presentation. Patti estimated 25 hours of work in that task, including normal travel time to the client's offices and other associated time spent. Thus, the module was priced at $875–simply a matter of multiplying the hourly rate by the total estimated hours.

There were other important factors to consider in setting up her fee schedule. Here are two, and the answers Patti came up with:

- *What about subcontractors—such as callers—she is asked to hire for some telephone sales projects?*

  Patti will hire an average caller at $8.00 an hour, and charge the client $12.00. A caller with technical product background may cost her $12.00 an hour, and Patti gets $18. The nominal markup is to cover her time for recruiting, training, and other details.

- *How are out-of-pocket expenses handled?*

  Any supplies acquired as part of client's program are billed to the company. Patti says these expenses are always foreseen, and preapproved by the client.

The fees and policies you finally decide on for your own business will depend on a multitude of factors. The important thing is to set your rates *realistically,* with an eye to your costs and what your local market will support.

The Anatomy of a
Successful Consulting Assignment

No two telephone sales consulting tasks are *exactly* alike, but most of them are basically similar, as pointed out earlier. The typical case, related for you below, has many parallels to situations that any consultant would frequently encounter. This particular one, conducted recently by a leading marketing firm, is accurately described for you in every detail:

THE CLIENT: A large, multi-line distributor of computer and electronic components operating west of the Rockies.

THE CLIENT'S NEED: An expanded customer base. The distributor's field salespeople were concentrating on *established* buyers due to time constraints. Some "pioneering" of new accounts occurred when advertising leads were followed up, but not enough to bring about significant expansion. It was felt that telephoning, aimed exclusively at a cold list of profiled prospects, would create the desired results.

THE CLIENT'S STRENGTHS: An on-hand inventory of components that usually took *weeks* for customers to get through other sources. The firm provided better field service than other sources could give. Finally, the firm made available to customers a series of user education programs, nonexistent through competitors.

THE CLIENT'S WEAKNESSES: Low visibility in the industry. A large number of potential customers never heard of the distributor—or knew the name but didn't have any awareness of what the company did. Some prospects preferred to buy direct from manufacturers, and that also presented an occasional problem. A third unfavorable element was the lack of calling facilities on the client's premises and marginal people resources to handle telephoning.

THE CLIENT'S SPECIFICATIONS: Qualify prospects from a cold list to the point where field salespeople would get relatively quick orders. This entailed the construction of a rather involved and lengthy question pattern, designed to dig out extensive data.

Aside from the desirability of mentioning the three client advantages outlined earlier, the marketing people also wanted a *group* of products described in every presentation that got past the qualification stage.

THE PROGRAM: The consultant would prepare the presentation and engage a caller who would operate from the consultant's offices. This would alleviate the space and people-power problems. Four hours per day of calling was planned in the initial stages, with an augmented schedule to follow when success had been proven.

HOW IT EVOLVED: For all the qualification questions, product information and customer benefits desired by the client, a reasonably streamlined presentation was developed. But when the caller tried it in actual practice, it proved overly cumbersome. The questions became confusing, and, while the pitch on three products plus various advantages didn't *appear* to be unwieldly on paper, it did turn out to be clumsy in actual cases.

In view of these findings, the consultant asked the client if the presentation could be simplified. He urged that the rigorous qualifications be altered, and the multi-product pitch be given only in certain cases. The three general advantages should be retained, but drastically condensed. Client approval was granted.

THE FINAL RESULTS: In the revised presentation, *the first question the caller asked was,* "Are you open for a bid on microcomputer memory products?" The answer rapidly filtered out the genuine prospects. From *that* point, the qualification proceeded more or less normally. Those who made it through the questions received a shortened product description that nicely got the point across in a matter of minutes.

This altered approach meant that field salespeople would have to call prospects and do a little of their own qualifying before taking the time for an appointment. This carefully constructed and meticulously fine-tuned program worked beautifully, producing at least six likely buyers per four hours of calling!

Putting Callers in Place
to Make Money By Remote Control

As in the above case, many companies quickly see the savings in having an outside firm supply callers, working space, facilities, and training. Very simply, it costs a fortune today for a corporation to recruit and train a new employee. They'd rather pay a consultant to handle it in many instances.

This is particularly true if a client wants to conduct calling for only three or four hours a day. You can obtain *one* good caller and have that person divide each day between two client-calling assignments. It's hard enough to find proficient full-time people, but part-timers are especially dif ficult to locate. Your client will usually jump at such a time-sharing opportunity.

What this means to you as a consultant is virtually *automatic ongoing income*. Once the initial presentation development is completed and a suitable caller is located and trained, you spend minimal time monitoring the program, and the income keeps rolling in for your share of the caller's hourly rate.

You probably recall that Patti marked up her caller rate 50 percent. *But there is no reason why a more substantial profit can't be tacked onto the hourly figure to cover overhead and other expenses.* Even at more substantial profit margins, two or three callers out working won't put you on easy street. But seven or eight will begin to generate nice dollars; at a conservative $4.50 per hour profit on each caller, eight will give you $36 an hour—or $216 for a six-hour day. And that's with *minimum* effort on your part once the programs are rolling smoothly!

In addition to your income on other aspects of your consulting activity, that is indeed a sweet extra—considering that your client pays for all the telephone expenses!

Compensation Programs That Get the Most Out of Telephone Pros

A client may occasionally ask you to suggest methods of paying callers. The question could be especially urgent if the company is planning to hire its own caller and has never gone through that process before.

It is not uncommon for a firm to unknowingly offer good telephone salespeople a straight salary on a par with clerical wages. In most cases it just won't work. Calling virtuosos have to be regarded as full-fledged members of the sales or marketing staff, and must be remunerated accordingly.

Most telephone sellers will shy away from *any* kind of locked-in salary, no matter how generous. They want the potential of reaching exceptionally high earnings for exceptional effort. At the same time, they *do* seem to prefer an assured base that will get them through slumps. So a nominal salary or draw, along with a comprehensive commission system, is generally the answer.

From the employer's point of view, an extremely heavy commission arrangement invites careless telephone qualifying and possibly high-pressure to force closes. A solid base salary combined with a commission or bonus system that *immediately* rewards increased sales is more likely to be comfortable for everybody.

By all means advise your client to model caller-pay programs after the company's *salespeople,* and *not* after the firm's administrative people.

The callers you engage to work in *your* office on client programs can also be given incentives. Either the client can be induced to participate in bonuses, or *you* can kick in to build incentives. Either way, the possibility of extra income assures an above-average effort.

As you gain valuable knowledge about the entire spectrum of telephone selling, you'll begin to discover new ways of disseminating that data for extra consulting income. Let's examine a few of those possibilities.

Seminars: One of Harvey O.'s
Fast Paths to Profitability

Most segments of American business seek knowledge today as never before. *The advantage in highly competitive industries will inevitably go to those firms that stay up with the latest ways to do things.* Therefore, progressive managers are constantly looking for ways to obtain useful information.

The information *you* command as an active telephone sales consultant is extremely saleable! It can be marketed via seminars, or through the preparation of specialized publications (covered later in this chapter). Harvey O., a consultant in a northwest U.S. city, does both. Here's his seminar approach.

● *Open seminars*

Harvey conducts one session every two months in a rented hotel conference room. The seminar runs one full day, and is designed for Marketing Managers and related positions. He charges $200 for the day, and includes a notebook that summarizes the total contents. Average attendance is 18 people. The financial breakdown usually looks like this:

Expenses

Room......................	$150.00
Notebooks....................	37.00
Coffee, etc.....................	50.00
Advertising.................	1,000.00
Miscellaneous.................	75.00
Total......................	$1,312.00

Gross receipts..............	$3,600.00
Net Profit	$2,288.00

Aside from the seminar income, Harvey has been able to convert around 10 percent of the attendees into full-fledged clients for his telephone consulting activities.

● *Customized in-house seminars*

Some client firms prefer to have a large group of employees attend a telephone sales seminar. At the same time, they like to have the contents customized to deal more specifically with their own products and policies.

In such a case, Harvey charges $2,200 for a five-hour session held on client premises. He spends two or three hours prior to the seminar customizing the normally general contents.

For either type of seminar, the consultant covers a list of topics that generally corresponds with this format:

    I. The Need for Telephone Selling Today

    II. Telephone Sales Applications

    III. Determining Best Approach for Your Product

    IV. Setting Up a Program

    V. Telephone Sales Management and Controls

    VI. How to Prepare and Use a Presentation

    VII. Effective Telephone Techniques

    VIII. Workshop (Role-Playing Session)

    IX. Question and Answer Period

The other half of this man's extra income comes from fast-selling telephone sales booklets.

Creating Your Own Money-Making Publications

By putting his knowledge and experience down in black and white, Harvey has easily created a completely separate profit-center that generates automatic income.

So far, he has developed the following informative booklets:

- *Effective Telephone Sales Techniques*
- *How to Build a Telephone Presentation*
- *Managing Your Telephone Sales Program*

Each publication runs just over 100 pages and represents a highly practical approach to the subject. Smaller businesses—those not inclined to use a consultant or devote a full day to a seminar—are the primary buyers.

Since Harvey does not trust his own ability to write, design, and oversee the production of the booklets, he engages the services of a college journalism student to polish the language, then has a printer coordinate the other steps to completion. His costs, including printing, total approximately $1.50 per book, and he sells them for $7.95 each.

A separate flyer publicizing the books accompanies his seminar mailers, and goes to key people in the companies on his client list. Harvey occasionally runs media ads inviting mail order, too. The consultant nets an average of $350 a month on book sales, so he's planning three others, plus an expanded advertising effort.

Here's another easy income technique for consultants.

Collecting and Selling
Valuable Market Intelligence By Telephone

Nearly every telephone sales consultant will receive inquiries from companies desiring market surveys. They don't want to sell anything during the call or even qualify in any way. They simply want to gather certain facts. The desired information might be used by a company for planning an advertising program, for new product development, for deciding on production levels, or for any number of other purposes. Needless to say, the average consultant welcomes this interesting business.

A midwest consultant goes one big step further to build his income when survey programs come along. As the details of the survey are being worked out with the client, this telephone specialist asks if he can use the expected input for his own purposes. The calls usually include five to ten questions, and the resulting answers can be most revealing in terms of market attitudes, buying patterns, brand accep-

tance, and other topics of exceptional importance to marketers.

*If the nature of the survey seems especially confidential
or sensitive, he doesn't ask if he can use the data.* But most of
these programs are designed to evoke general information
and opinions about user sentiments, and are *not* confidential.

The consultant promises not to name companies, products, people's names, or any other specifics. He is usually
granted permission to use statistics, plus many facts and
figures, *if the sources are not identified.*

In the course of an average year, this enterprising consultant can put together two or three market reports that
turn out to be extremely valuable to ad agencies, publishers,
manufacturers, and other companies in search of valid information. A typical collection of survey results will go for
$250. It's a very neat way of turning cold numbers into nice
cash profits!

Preparing Proposals That Sell Your Services

Any salesperson or entrepreneur who deals with larger
companies is intimately familiar with the formal proposal. It
is really nothing more than an elaborate description of services you are prepared to render, along with a quotation of
fees for those services. While that is the bare-bones *intent* of
a proposal, the one that will truly do a job for you has to be
much more than merely a rundown of what you'll do and how
much you charge to do it.

The fact is, your proposal is very often your only "representative" in a company you want as a client. You have one
opportunity to present your telephone program on a face-to-
face basis. The people you talk to like what you tell them
about your services, and invariably ask for a proposal that
restates your proposition. They can now run this document
past advertising, a few V.P.'s who have to approve it, plus the
President.

Unfortunately, your initial contacts in the firm can't be expected to sell your plan to the others as eloquently as *you* do, so the selling punch must somehow be built into your proposal. It has to be a document that goes a long way toward rekindling the same enthusiasm *you* were able to spark; that means it is much more than a fancy price quotation!

The elements of an effective proposal are described below.

● *Section I: Overview*

Give a brief statement about the general situation; for example, why the prospective client needs your services, and perhaps a line or two about circumstances prevailing in the market that tend to make a telephone sales program timely and wise.

● *Section II: (your company) Background*

Now you tell the reader why your services are right for the job. If possible, tie specific attributes or experiences of yours to the client's perceived needs, as pointed out in Section I. It helps to be able to say you've done successful programs similar to the one being proposed.

● *Section III: Objectives*

Here, you *quantify* what you realistically feel will be accomplished. If possible, use conservative numbers to show anticipated closing ratios, sales increases, etc. *Always* keep the objectives closely aligned with the prospect's stated goals for telephone sales. Keep it relevant!

● *Section IV: Work Statement*

This part shows how you intend to accomplish the objectives outlined in Section III. Go through a description of each step you recommend for the firm, in order of when the event will take place. For example, preparing the presentation may happen first, followed by the training of callers two weeks later, and so forth.

Handle each service module as a separate paragraph in your proposal, and include a timetable that shows the date when each part starts and finishes. If you're not certain of the date, at least indicate estimated elapsed time for every segment.

In this Section, *avoid open-ended sentences!* Tighten the definition of your responsibility so there is absolutely *no* room for misunderstanding by the client. Don't use tentative words like "about," "approximately," or "if." Be exceedingly specific! Spell out, in the most definite possible terms, what you will deliver.

● *Section V: Fees and Terms*

Show the dollars and cents you charge for each module you recommend for the prospective client. Show the total tab, and finish by stating your payment terms. Here again, be specific. Don't hide even a penny. If you have to guess at variables such as expected telephone bills, estimate on the high side, but not before you do a little research.

One last bit of advice: Keep it as brief as possible, *but be thorough.*

Whether you *do* pursue your own telephone sales consultancy business—or prefer to oversee a calling operation for an employer—the following management guidelines should prove invaluable.

a mini-management manual for telephone sales professionals 14

Whether you work as a caller for yourself or an employer . . . manage a telephone sales operation . . . or consult with companies . . . you have to understand the basics of sound supervisory steps to achieve your goals.

The following pages describe management steps that leading telephone experts have selected as being most important to getting a solid program off to a flying start, and *keeping* it there. Some of the points have been covered to some extent in earlier chapters. But in this section they are viewed strictly from the manager's vantage point. As you will see, most of these topics center on the *people* aspects of a calling effort. That, after all, is what selling is all about!

Evaluating Telephone Selling Techniques

The underlying concern of management is to assure that the goals for a telephone sales program remain strongly in focus until there is adequate justification to modify them.

On a periodic basis, those objectives should be reevaluated. The answers to questions like these will reveal whether a program is on track:

- Can orders be *closed* by telephone, or is the desired purpose to *qualify* prospects? If prospect qualification is preferred, can a field visit be arranged by phone on the first call, or is it more practical to set the stage for a further telephone call before contact by a field sales representative?

- Can telephone sales be applied to both incoming *and* outgoing calls (if it is not being so utilized now)? Can the program be of value in customer service or other departments?

- Are there *specific* information needs that can be gathered during telephone sales calls that can benefit the company?

A review like this should be made *at least every three months*. The answers will sometimes prompt changes in the basic direction of a program, or in the dialogue callers are using. Here are some guidelines for making changes.

Making Adjustments to Enhance Results

Changes have to be made to the presentation from time to time in order to keep it in-step with realities in the marketplace and to fit it to the personalities of various callers. But these changes should not be made without due deliberation of the managers responsible for the telephone program.

There are two basic types of change that will be inevitable:

- *Alterations to the verbatim script*. This, in most instances, occurs automatically as callers talk to prospects. Since virtually *every* salesperson will evolve toward words and phrases that fit his or her personality, you probably won't find it feasible to *formalize* those little changes unless someone comes up with a vastly superior way of delivering a certain point.

Your main task here is to assure that the *basic integrity* of the presentation is retained. As you know, language can convey distorted messages when key words are dropped or modified, so it pays to frequently listen in on callers to be sure major changes are not taking place.

● *Alterations to the basic strategy.* Changes to steps in the presentation logic flow should be considered more carefully than small adjustments to words here and there. If these larger modifications to presentation structure seem to make sense in theory, they should be *tested* before being adopted.

In monitoring calls, be sure all presentation steps are used in *sequence.* Callers will sometimes inadvertently skip key steps, then fall into a pattern of delivery that leads to slumps.

Defining Caller's Specific Job Functions

One of the most frustrating situations to some callers is when they are asked to perform tasks unrelated to their primary responsibilities. The fact is, certain people can adapt to frequent diversions from their usual tasks. Others find it extremely distracting and don't function well under fluid, unstructured conditions.

Solid management procedure is to define in detail the *expected* role of a caller. A typical weekly workload or description of chores must be realistically estimated. This definition should be formulated *before* the first candidates for a calling job are interviewed since it is important for you to convey at least a general idea about what the position entails.

Set up a typical caller's week. While it may not be essential at the start-up to come up with specific sales quotas, it is important to establish expectations for the total number of calls that should be made, plus details like the ones listed here:

- Daily hours.
- Reports that have to be completed, and other necessary clerical chores associated with the job.
- Reporting lines; who to talk with when things are needed or questions have to be answered.
- Overtime that may be required.
- Frequency of performance reviews, and thorough explanation of the compensation program and incentive plan, if any.

Also consider any other factors that directly or indirectly impact the individual's work environment.

When making your selection of qualified applicants, take extra care to assure that the finalists have the ability and desire to conform to *your* methods of operation. More about that right now.

Insisting That Callers Adapt
to New Methods and Procedures

Many employers prefer to hire experienced callers. The usual pattern is that these people worked in other telephone operations and are considered "pros." The apparent benefit is a shorter learning curve, greater poise early in the job, and so forth.

To a certain extent these advantages are real. But whether they compensate for the shortcomings inherent with many deeply experienced callers is another question indeed. The following checklist might help a manager come to a conclusion:

- Will the experienced caller utilize *your* prescribed phone techniques, or fall back to more familiar ones that may not do justice to your project or service?
- Will this person conform to *your* company policies, or disdain them in favor of more familiar guidelines carried over from a prior business association?

- If old methods and rules *are* favored over the ones you wish to impose, will the veteran caller attempt to convert your *other* telephone salespeople to their way of thinking?

The arbitrary rejection of all previously experienced callers is extremely limiting to you and unfair to applicants. But the hiring of a person who possesses ingrained habits—and is hopelessly attached to a different employment life-style—can present a management problem.

Your forming staff has to accept the systems *you* prescribe, and the level of cooperation *you* establish! There is always room for variation within those parameters in order to preserve individuality. But can your company live with wide departures from your methods and approaches? It's a question only individual managers can answer for themselves.

As soon as staffing is completed, implementation follows. Here are some management tips for the all-important training function.

How to Conduct Initial and Ongoing Training Sessions

At least one full day of initial training should be provided before a caller's first contact with a prospect. The telephone presentation is the core of your training. By going through the presentation from start to finish and discussing each section in sequence, it all falls nicely into place. One more half-day can be devoted to covering general call techniques.

As an ongoing program, just one formal training session per month will guarantee the growth of your telephone salespeople into highly accomplished specialists. In these one to two-hour meetings, time is devoted *entirely* to discussion of sales strategies and techniques. If you have a number of callers, open discussion about various strategies is valuable. It brings out different points of view and demonstrates diverse ways to solve problems.

Productive training depends to a large part on preparation. These steps are recommended:

- Select no more than two topics for any one training session. Examples are handling objections and trial closes.

- Prepare some kind of visual support in advance. This might consist of pages excerpted from a pertinent article, charts, etc. Visuals do a tremendous job of reinforcing a verbal delivery.

- Plan to talk about your chosen topics for 15 to 20 minutes, then open the subjects up to general discussion or debate, as the case may be. *Work from notes so your session flows smoothly.*

- If practical, schedule topics that seem to be problem areas. *Closing* is always a beneficial subject, and can stand to be repeated from time to time.

- Ask your callers what *they* would like to cover in the next training session. They'll always identify areas that need work.

The Crucial Transition from Training to Calling

As soon as you feel that a caller has an adequate grasp of the presentation steps, the various control forms, and other components of the telephone sales program, kickoff time has come. It may be helpful to condense the presentation logic flow and corresponding dialogue into a one-page summary that the caller can use as a speedy guide. Figure 14-1 shows how it's done.

In addition to the one-page summary, anything else you

Merge the presentation steps in your logic flow . . .

with *key phrases* taken from the dialogue you have prepared . . .

and *combine* them. The result is a *one-page summary* you can quickly consult during calls. It helps you remain *natural and relaxed* while calling, and keeps you solidly on the track toward a close.

The key phrases are *reminders* of what each step consists of, and spare you the task of searching through heavy dialogue during calls.

Figure 14-1

can do to make the transition from training to calling smooth and natural, the better. The objective, of course, is to eliminate any feeling a caller may have that he or she is being abruptly "thrown out of the nest." An hour or two of closely supervised calls can help provide such a smooth transition. These closely supervised calls are "live" contacts with prospects. Each one is thoroughly discussed *before and after* a call is made.

For example, before making a call, the prospect is evaluated in terms of *known facts;* what is he or she likely to purchase? Why? Who would the principal contact be? What are the "hot buttons" of that person likely to be? What k   .d of objections may arise? (Plus other expected characteristics.)

The new caller then goes into action and contacts the prospect. An extensive critique or discussion follows every call during this supervised session. With a manager present, the caller can be expected to be more self-conscious than usual. Add this to the fact that it's the first actual use of the presentation, and you have a set of circumstances that are not conducive to optimum results. So the *strategic* facets of the conversation should be noted, and *not* just the technique aspects.

Regardless of the outcome of the supervised calls, criticism should be *gentle and constructive.* Normally, the delivery of each succeeding call improves markedly, and by that afternoon the caller is ready to work independently with complete confidence. This closely monitored use of the prepared presentation goes a long way toward making it second nature to even an inexperienced caller.

A manager who is accustomed to dealing with clients and prospects can accelerate the learning process by *alternating* the calls with the new employee. The trainee then has an opportunity to hear an experienced person use the presentation. These calls, too, should be discussed before and after to derive as much benefit as possible from the dialogue that actually took place.

Establishing Operating Guidelines
for Your Caller

Striking a good balance between "the rules of the game" and total operating freedom can be difficult. On the one hand, you can't expect good performance if a caller is encumbered with a long list of "do's" and "don'ts." On the other hand, a completely free-form operating environment doesn't often work, either.

A little time during the first day should be set aside for explaining general company rules that would effect your callers. These few minutes not only help assure that each person dovetails into the overall scheme of things, but they also make your telephone salespeople feel like part of the team.

Try to avoid taking *anything* for granted. A basic point like what the working hours are, or when lunch is taken, or which exits to use, might be unknown to a new person.

Ideal Manager/Caller Interface

Good salespeople are not necessarily easy to get along with, to supervise, or to regiment tightly. They *are* good sellers because they are expressive, independent, and proud. The same characteristics that make them abstract thinkers can make them mediocre reporters of fact. A strong sales corps, whether it functions in field or telephone sales, cannot usually be put into a regimentation designed for accountants, engineers, or people of distinctly different orientation. In view of the typical salesperson's personality profile, a certain type of management style works better than others.

Maximum freedom of movement should be allowed. Along with that, breaks can be more frequent. The manager's primary concern is this: By the day's end, are the *total calls* at an acceptable level?

The ideal interpersonal relationship between a manager and caller is warm and casual, but marked by a tacit understanding that quotas *must be delivered*. A stiff and formal relationship does not make for satisfactory dealings over the long haul.

While a loose, free-flowing association is desirable, it should never be allowed to get in the way of a supervisor's ability to criticize or discipline a caller, when necessary. An ideal telephone sales manager is informal on the surface, but rock-solid business beneath that top layer.

Effective Critique Methods
That Sharpen Performance

Criticism of a caller's methods is, in concept, a constructive activity. But in reality, it is exceedingly hard on one's self-esteem. The truly good salesperson is sensitive and usually does not respond well to criticism, no matter how constructive it is *meant* to be. Nevertheless, a manager has to conduct personal critiques periodically—at least on a monthly basis. The following method is used successfully by experienced sales managers.

Combine criticism with equal measures of genuine recognition for the caller's accomplishments during a given time period. *Try not to criticize unless you first relate a good point.* For example:

"I think your product description is one of the best
I've heard. Let's see if we can find a way to make
your *close* just as strong!"

This puts your comment on a *purely positive note*. Before you tear down, you do a little building up.

It helps tremendously to use "our," "we," and "us" instead of "you" in describing a problem. As the manager, you are then *sharing* the obligation to improve and grow. You are *part* of the operation, *not* merely an aloof outsider point ing an accusing finger.

How to Plan and Conduct Successful Meetings

While we're on the subject of caller morale, it's timely to discuss the impact general meetings can have on the attitudes of telephone salespeople. The all-too common perception that callers are concerned only with the block of work that has been laid out for the next eight hours is erroneous in most instances. They *are* interested in the progress of the program as a whole; the follow-up of field sales (if applicable); the implication of their efforts on other parts of the company, and so forth. Good callers really do *want to see the big picture!*

Therefore, a general progress report is ideal subject matter for meetings held on a weekly basis. The tone is decidedly upbeat, and the conclusion of the session can be opened up to questions and discussion—as long as the total time of this general meeting is held to one hour or less (since it is ideally held first thing Monday morning).

This particular get-together should never be used as a forum for airing individual problems or grievances. The latter areas are *always* covered during individual critiques (discussed earlier) scheduled toward the end of the workweek. The rationale for this late-in-the-week time slot is to give the caller a weekend to get the criticism in proper perspective and to get revitalized. Then, the Monday general meeting *builds* enthusiasm before calling begins for the week. As with any other meeting, the telephone sales manager prepares an agenda for this session, complete with notes that assure thorough coverage of the selected topics.

Setting Quotas and Enforcing Them

In actual time sequence, a rock-solid quota usually cannot be properly established as early as on program kickoff day. There is no precedent to use as a performance index at that stage. Even if a prior caller *had* generated certain sales figures, it is usually an injustice (to you *and* the new caller) to use those old numbers as a basis for your expectations.

There is nothing so discouraging to a salesperson than constantly falling short of a quota that seems to be based more on management optimism than on reality. The number has to be *reasonable* and *reachable*.

When all quotas for callers have been selected and adjusted to everyone's comfort, the very serious question of enforcement must be addressed. A quota is utterly meaningless unless it is accompanied by a system of incentives and penalties.

A caller who consistently exceeds quota is either putting forth extraordinary effort—was originally underrated —or both. Perhaps, too, the quota was not realistic. The manager has to make a judgment about which situation exists, and act accordingly. If a bonus is to be paid for meeting or exceeding quota, it is advisable to pay it even if the expected sales level is suspect. An adjustment can be made later, *but credibility has to be protected at all costs!*

A caller who *never* makes the required number is either laying down on the job—was originally overrated—or both. Here again, maybe the quota has no basis in reality. If *visible* work output from the person appears to be adequate, it probably pays to further adjust the quota downward and see what happens. If figures *still* aren't met, most managers would consider replacing the caller.

Monitoring Follow-Up
Efficiency and Effectiveness

The other facet of a manager's responsibility in assuring overall sales fulfillment is in the area of inquiry follow-up. If a particular prospect asks for a quotation on products or services, the system must guarantee that (1) the quotation itself is prepared and communicated back to the prospect quickly, and (2) that a timely call-back is made for the purpose of securing the order.

All prospects who express above-average interest, but cannot make buying commitments during the initial contact for one reason or another, *have to be called again at a specific time in the near future.*

A significant volume of sales come out of follow-up calls, yet it is by and large a chaotic aspect of most sales systems, as pointed out more than once in this book. Since the telephone sales manager remains close to the physical calling activity—and to the various prospect files—a *frequent* spot-check of follow-up activity is a quick and extremely positive way to assure it is being handled properly.

Take the following steps once every several weeks:

- Review all Prospect Forms for a period of one week, before they are filed. Note the date they are scheduled for follow-up. Use *one future day* as the basis of your spot-check.

  For example, if a total of seven inquiries in that group are scheduled for call-backs on Wednesday, September 11, *that will be your day to see if those seven have, indeed, been contacted as planned.*

  At the end of the day on Wednesday, you ask the caller for a rundown of all follow-up calls made that day. The seven specifically identified prospects should, of course, be in that number. If not, deal with the problem during the monthly *personal critique* session.

- The other step is for the purpose of seeing that follow-ups are being properly scheduled.

  At the end of that same Wednesday, ask the caller to consult the line on the Daily Call Tally Sheet for the day just passed. Ask for a rundown of each contact that had been scheduled for a later call-back. Each of these follow-ups should be slotted in the proper place, under "Hot" or "Warm," in the caller's Prospect File. If so, you can have reasonable assurance that those future follow-ups will be made.

Also, check the corresponding Prospect Forms for each of these inquiries to be sure that the correct follow-up date was entered in the Activity Section of the form. In checking for follow-up effectiveness, there is simply no alternative to *personally* making sample calls to randomly selected inquiries. You will find out if promised actions have been taken by your callers, and if the relationships have been handled professionally.

A Model Management Agenda
for Three Months

Figure 14-2 illustrates a theoretical calendar of events that a telephone sales manager might follow to assure the execution of all required control steps.

The outstanding benefit in maintaining this type of agenda is that it provides close control of the telephone sales program, but is *not* excessively demanding in terms of time given to the program.

Above all, *fit your preferred style and approach* to the overall management task. In fact, all the information in this book is subject to *your personal interpretation*. Invariably, five different salespeople or managers will come up with five different (but strongly related) ways to go about handling one strategy!

By all means, remain a distinct individual, and let your own unique personality be the leading feature in your ability to deal with and pursuade others.

Equally important, use this book as a constant reference. There is *no* reason why you or any other reader cannot be as proficient and successful as the telephone sales pros quoted in its chapters. All it takes is an understanding of the mechanics of the strategies, plus a little practice!

EXAMPLE OF A TELEPHONE SALES
MANAGEMENT AGENDA (THREE MONTHS)

AUGUST

Monday	Tuesday	Wednesday	Thursday	Friday
DESCRIBE CO. GUIDELINES – PLUS TRAINING	HALF-DAY TRAINING – START CALLING	WORK OUT FIELD SALES FOLLOW-UP LOOP	REVIEW PRESENTATION	
GENERAL MEETING	ESTABLISH QUOTAS	GROUP TRAINING		
GENERAL MEETING				
GENERAL MEETING				PERSONAL CRITIQUES

SEPTEMBER

Monday	Tuesday	Wednesday	Thursday	Friday
START TEST		GROUP TRAINING		
GENERAL MEETING		CHECK PROGRAM OBJECTIVES		
GENERAL MEETING	REVISE QUOTAS			
GENERAL MEETING		REVIEW BACK-UP DATA		SPOT-CHECK FOLLOW-UP
				PERSONAL CRITIQUES

OCTOBER

Monday	Tuesday	Wednesday	Thursday	Friday
GENERAL MEETING		GROUP TRAINING	REVIEW PRESENTATION	END TEST
GENERAL MEETING			CHECK FIELD SALES FOLLOW-UP	
GENERAL MEETING				
GENERAL MEETING				PERSONAL CRITIQUES

Figure 14-2

closing notes for power-selling by telephone

This brief closing statement relates a few sobering facts that I hope will underscore the importance of telephone selling to you. Early in this book, it is reported that the average field sales visit costs about $150 today. Since "averages" rarely tell the whole story, that particular subject warrants a closer look.

Some high-technology firms conduct field sales calls that demand the involvement of not only a field salesperson, but a highly trained engineer or systems analyst as well. Such companies claim a *$300 to $600 per-visit cost*. At the other extreme, the operator of a small, independent business simply can't make a personal call to a prospect for much less than $100.

Those per-call expenses are alarming enough, but suddenly assume mind-boggling proportions when you consider the following data, compiled through a recent survey conducted on a national scale:

Typically, it takes from 3.8 to 4.9* personal sales visits to obtain one close!

The high-technology company could easily spend well over $1,500 on sales calls alone for an order. The "average" firm invests about $450 on these interviews leading to a sale, and even the smallest organization has to be ready to lay out somewhere in the neighborhood of $300 for one close!

Those realistic figures tell me—and I trust tell you— that *every seller has to become a telephone professional to survive in the 1980s.* And the sooner the better.

Reaching your market economically and effectively *demands* that you link an intelligently planned and cost-effective advertising program to a carefully structured and efficient telephone selling campaign.

Seibly S. Buffum, Vice President
BLD/Doremus West
Advertising ● Public Relations

---

*Source: McGraw-Hill Publications Co.

index